# DON'T ASK DON'T GET

# DON'T ASK
# DON'T GET

**Steve Grayson**
With Frances Kavanagh

First published in Great Britain in 2008
By KavanaghTipping Publishing
Wingham, Kent
CT3 1AR

For Jeannette
Without your strength and courage, where would I
be?


For my lovely daughter, Laura,
my wonderful grandchildren, Ben and Grace,


&
of course,
Sunny.

# Contents

Author's note: This is a memoir; certain names and geographical locations have been changed to protect the privacy of individuals.

# Preface

There's an expression in the newspaper trade: *turning someone over,* meaning befriending someone, gaining a measure of their trust to get information from them, and then turning round and exposing their secrets. As a photojournalist and an investigator, that's what I do for the most part - turn people over. I infiltrate the hidden places, the secret corners, the cracks in the façade called civilization, and bring them into focus. To do that, I have to pretend to be someone I'm not or bullshit my way in and out of situations to get the story - being an undercover liar is part of my job and I'm good at it.

I've also lied a lot in my working life outside journalism. No excuses - it has all been about survival, clawing my way out of the slums, taking care of my family and getting on. In the absence of advantages, I used whatever I had – confidence and the gift of the gab. If you don't use what you've been given, it'll drop off, and I'm passionate about getting off your arse, getting on and enjoying life. I have no patience with whinging people who don't try and say, 'I can't ...'.

I make no secret of the way I've lived my life: everything in this book is true, to the best of my knowledge and memory; otherwise, I would be lying to myself. I don't do that because I have a profound belief in myself and have always remained true to that.

I've observed, documented, engaged in life more than most people would ever want to. And I've paid my dues: life has turned *me* over more than once!

# 1
# Stephen Moses

I have been involved in countless investigations, some of which I am not at liberty to talk about, and many of which have become a jumble of memories running into each other, but I can never forget the innocent who get drawn into situations through no fault of their own, especially children.

In South America, many years ago, I met Miguel, a young boy who lived with his grandfather. He was one of the more fortunate: he had a home in a place where thousands of children still fight for basic survival, working the streets - selling drugs or their bodies - or working for different gangs as runners.

The demand for drugs in the West also forces the poor, like Miguel's grandfather, to work in factories that produce cocaine. Miguel took me to the one where his grandfather worked, one day, and we climbed onto some old petrol barrels so that I could get a better look into the compound where about two dozen men were standing in a circle – farmers, Miguel said. They were a pretty shabby bunch, some with guns, but they seemed quite relaxed. There was a man in the centre of the circle, weighing bags of cocaine, and standing beside him was a girl of no more than twelve. She had long black hair and the dark, intense eyes of a woman twice her age. Miguel explained that she was writing the weights of the cocaine on a piece of paper, which then became a receipt that she would give to the cocaine farmer.

A police officer stood the other side of her, overseeing the proceedings. I thought it was strange that he didn't have a gun, but then I saw that every time one of the farmers received a receipt from the little girl, the police officer walked over, took the receipt and gave him another one. The police were keeping a tally and taking a piece of the action.

Petrol and chemical fumes permeated the air, making Miguel's eyes and nose stream, as he told me in his broken English that his grandfather had worked in the factory for as long as he could remember, and his grandmother had died two years previously, after contracting a chest infection.

'Nobody help her,' he said. 'Nobody care.' The tears that ran down his grubby face were not caused by the fumes this time: they came from his broken heart.

We were soon spotted and Miguel ran away as a man with a gun came over and told me to leave. I walked away from that unbearable factory and into the fresh air, worrying about Miguel and his grandfather, and hoping that my short visit would not cause trouble for them and make their lives even harder.

The media shows misery happening everyday across the globe, but an image can never have the impact of a flesh and blood child standing inches away.

If he survived, Miguel is a man now, but whenever I remember my childhood, the child who was Miguel stands beside me, showing me that though I did not have much, I had everything.

My mother's name was Minnie Eliza and she was an amazing, beautiful lady: strong, hardworking and generous. Her father was a full time soldier who had fought in the Boer War, the Crimea War, and in India during the uprising. In the First World War, he got shrapnel in the head, which damaged his brain and he died soon after. There is nothing to show for all those decades of service to this country except a little metal plaque, which everybody got, saying: *Sorry for your loss, for King and Country.*

Her mother remarried, and Minnie Eliza Goom left home and went into service, because her stepfather was a drunkard and she did not like him. I never knew either of those grandparents.

She was always called Min, and she was twenty three and pregnant with my eldest sister, Eileen, when she and my father got married in 1930. After Eileen came Sam, Ray, Janet and, finally, me; she loved us all to distraction. We lived in rooms in a big house in Kilburn. I was born in the front room sixty one years ago and took a long time about it, so I'm told. Family legend has it that I was called Stephen after a jockey my father liked. Dad was partial to a little betting and quite often put sixpence each way on a horse. He won quite a bit, by all accounts, and always gave it to my mum.

Before I was born, the family lived in three rooms with an outside toilet and no running water; they got water from a shared washhouse in the back yard. Soon after I arrived, my parents rented an additional room upstairs when the previous occupant died. That room had a tiny corner sink in it with a cold-water tap. Luxury!

Despite the inadequate washing facilities, Mum kept it so spotless you could have eaten off the floor, and even though everywhere was falling to pieces outside, she always cleaned the front step. We all had to be clean too; we might not have had the best clothes in the world, but we had to be clean or she would not let us out. I'd clean my shoes and she'd say 'Not only the front, Stephen!' because the backs had to be clean and so did the part underneath between the sole and the heel. We also had to have white vests; if they were slightly grey, we had to take them off and she would wash them again in the washhouse, where my father had built a big 'copper'. You put water in a big copper bowl on top of a concrete oven, where coal or any old rubbish was burned, and the fire would heat the water. My mum would put all the clothes in it, twist and turn them until the water boiled, and then put them through the mangle. (In later years, we bought her a washing machine, but she wouldn't turn it on; she didn't like it. 'How can it be washing things?' she said. 'It doesn't boil.')

I think her attention to cleanliness was one of the few ways she had of looking after us and keeping us healthy. The living conditions were very poor and there were horrendous drainage problems under the houses, which caused a terrible smell, but nothing was done about it. They had been on the list for a council house for years before I was born, but did not get one until I was thirteen, and only then because the houses in our street were being demolished. When my brothers and sisters were growing up, they

4

got every childhood disease there was, including scarlet fever, and the whole family, including Mum and Dad, got diphtheria. I was lucky to have come along later.

For bathing, we had a tin bath and everyone took a turn in front of the fire. I was in it every day and I used to listen to 'Journey Into Space' on the wireless, which was a treat for me. My dad ran a football team and the whole team would sometimes walk in on me, teasing and embarrassing me, telling my mum to put the kettle on, and there she'd be with ten or eleven blokes to deal with, as if she didn't have anything else to do. It was hectic in our house – always something happening - but she didn't care; she coped with everything. I don't know how she lived so long or did such a good job of looking after us all, except that she was very strong willed and it was a way of life. She had never had money but she just got on with things, she was always happy and singing. Everyone liked her.

There was also a neighbourhood bathhouse, Granville Road Baths, where we sometimes went for a bath. Mum also did her washing there when it got too much and she had the whole football team's kit to wash. She would take it there in a pram, wash it all by hand, put it through the mangle and then dry it in the driers, which were like big cupboards: you opened the door, pulled out a rack, hung the clothes on it, pushed it back in and closed the door; after that, she would iron it all. The irons were plugged into the ceiling and there would be thirty or forty wires hanging like vertical, wriggling worms attached to all the women ironing in a line, sweat pouring off them in this awful, monstrous-size room full of steam,

5

while their sons or husbands were all having baths. Mum always had terrible bruises on her legs from falling over buckets that people left all over the place.

I started going with her when I was seven or eight. She would hand me over to a man who took me into the men's section and ran a bath for me. They were huge baths: I couldn't see over the top; I'd look up and just see the ceiling. You got a bar of Lifebuoy soap, which you had to give back afterwards, and Mum would give me a towel because she would never let me use theirs. All the baths were in separate cubicles, and there were big stopcocks outside each door that were operated by the attendants; you could hear all the taps going and people shouting for more hot in number six, more cold in number three and so on. As I got older, I'd go with my mates and we'd mess about: I'd shout for more hot in whatever number bath one of them was in, he'd yelp and swear at me and shout for more cold in another number, hoping it was mine. It was fun.

My dad, Sam, was Jewish; our surname was Moses before he changed it to Grayson when I was thirteen. He was one of sixteen children, not all of whom survived, but the extended family is huge. There were massive family gatherings when I was a child, where people I didn't know would come up saying 'Is this little Stevie?'. Those gatherings were fascinating; I loved them because everyone had a tale to tell.

I have a picture of my grandparents, with eleven of their children, hanging in our house and some years ago we needed one of our ceilings plastered. Jeannette, my wife, rang round and arranged for a plasterer to come. While he was working, he suddenly turned to Laura, my daughter, who happened to be in the room. 'How come you've got a picture of my grandfather and my family on your wall?' he asked in amazement.

'No, that's my dad's grandparents,' she told him.

'Hang on! Those are *my* grandparents! Those are *my* uncles!'

Surreal! His name is Moss – not so far removed from Moses – and he turned out to be a relative I never knew I had. It's strange how life works!

Our great grandparents emigrated from the Ukraine and were given the name *Moses* on arrival here. As families with unpronounceable names came into this country, they were often given names connected to something about them or what they did: names like Tailor, for instance, were common. My great grandparents undoubtedly got the name Moses because they were Jewish.

My grandfather was born in Whitechapel and worked in salvage then later in antiques. He also used to sell chaffinches, which the family had gone to the countryside and caught.

My father, however, did not do so well, and was always under a lot of financial pressure. He was a French polisher by trade, but he worked for his uncle as a painter and decorator, and although he had worked for him for a long time, he never received any preferential treatment. He suffered with terrible migraines and if he was too sick to work he was not paid: he only got paid for what he did. Consequently, if he could stand up, he went to work, ill or not. He got a badly infected leg one time, and the doctor told him he had to rest it because the infection was spreading, and he could lose the leg. Of course, there was no money coming in and no help from the relatives, so Mum had to go to the social assistance office. At first, they also refused any help. The uncle Dad worked for was a builders' merchant, and the assistance people, knowing there was money in the family, assumed we must be getting help. When my mum said we weren't, they actually phoned and asked my uncle. He confirmed that he was not helping us – because, according to him, my dad was 'only a cousin' - and my mum was given food coupons, the value of which had to be paid back once my dad was working again. This reduced my mum to tears because she had a lot of pride and she knew that when she went to the shops everyone would know the plight we were in. The stress of all that for both my parents was enormous.

I felt my father was less devoted to me because I was an 'accident', coming along seven years after Janet. I felt distant from him, and, to this day, I don't feel that I ever really knew him. I know he loved me, but he never showed it and didn't have a lot of contact with me, other than with his hand! He used to hit me round the head, which was normal in those days, although my sisters used to yell at him not to do it. He was not a nasty person, but he was under so much unrelenting pressure, and I was always up to something.

As I got older, I would want to hit him back, but out of respect I never would and neither would my brothers, even though he was short and we all grew taller than him, taking after our mother. One of the many times he had a go at Ray, who was more of a rascal than me, they argued and he went to hit Ray, who ducked, and my father hit a cupboard with a mirror on the front, shattered the glass, and cut his hand so badly he had to be taken to hospital.

Always struggling to make ends meet, naturally, he would not stand for any food being wasted, and, after a particular incident one day, it's something I'm never likely to forget. The fish man came with his horse and cart every Sunday and my mum bought winkles, which we had for tea with bread and butter. On this particular day, I wanted to go out to play, so I pretended I'd eaten all my food, hid the bread under the table, asked Mum if I could go, and off I went. When they were clearing up, they found the bread. It might have only been a quarter of a sandwich, but my dad gave me such a thrashing, shouting 'We can't afford for you to put bread on the floor!' I can still hear him saying it. To him, throwing food away was a crime.

He did love football and had a membership in Queens Park Rangers because he knew the team when they played in Queens Park – a little park at the time – and he always supported them. The football team he ran was recruited from the local pub, the Albert. My father didn't drink – he'd have lemonade with maybe a touch of beer - but the team had meetings in the pub.

They used to play at Stonebridge Park, about nine miles away from where we lived, and we would go in a big, old, army lorry that one of the blokes had. I was only little, a mascot of sorts, and I took the collection box round for donations towards keeping up the ground and paying the fees to play there. I was also handy for retrieving the ball: there was a circus storage place next to the pitch, fenced with barbed wire, and the ball would inevitably go over. When this happened, one fellow would get on another's shoulders, pick me up and put me over to go and get it. One day, when I was about seven, instead of being lifted back I wanted to go meandering around the storage place to look at the big wooden animals and the strong man with his dumb bells, where you hit the base of the stand and caused a weight to go up, measuring your strength. The guys left me to it, and I got carried away, playing on everything, until it started getting dark. I went back to the fence and they'd gone! I was terrified because I was too little to climb out.

All the footballers used to go back to our house, take off their kit and give it to my mum to wash. (She had all that to do by hand – thick mud and grass stains - because it was my dad's team.) When they got back to Kilburn, this time, my mum, fortunately, asked where I was. Of course, they immediately drove like mad back to Stonebridge and I could hear them calling me. I was yelling 'Yay-Yay, help me!' to my brother, Ray. That's what I called him when I was very little, and when I was very nervous I'd go back to it.

A similar thing had actually happened to him, too. Mum had taken him round in his pram to the Home and Colonial, which was a chain of grocery shops. She was rushing to get dinner on the table and it was not until everyone was sitting down to eat that someone asked where Ray was. 'Oh my god!' shrieked Mum. 'I've left him at the Home and Colonial!' She went running back and there he was, still sitting outside the shop in his pram.

Mum was always rushing because she left everything until the last minute. Before she did the daily food shopping, she had a routine – making beds and so on - and it was always a race to get the dinner on the table. Everybody would be home at midday, waiting. It used to cause arguments with my dad, especially on a Saturday when he wanted to get to the football match. But that was Mum, and they are the only arguments I can remember them having; they were very happy together.

I shared a bedroom and a double bed with my brothers. Then, when I got a bit older, my parents bought me a single bed of my own. My brothers were supposed to continue to share the double bed, but a bed to yourself was a treat. When they came home from seeing their girlfriends, whoever was in first would gently lift me out and put me in the double bed. Which one of us got the single bed became the luck of the draw. One night, I filled up the enamel potty (potties go with outside toilets!) with water and balanced it on top of the door so that whoever walked in first would get soaked, I'd wake up and stop them from moving me. I went to sleep, happy and oblivious, but it was my dad who walked in! The pot nearly knocked him out, and, to add insult to injury, he thought he'd been dowsed in urine. I got a good hiding!

We were just rascals. Neither of my parents drank, but there was a pub called the Neville, where my mother used to work at weekends. She always looked very pretty when she curled her hair, put on her one good dress and went to work 'at the bar', as she called it, because she thought that made it sound like a solicitor's office. Anyway, she took me there once to look around. In the back yard there were piles and piles of empty bottles and I asked her why they were there. 'People bring them back and get threepence on them, then the bottles are taken away, washed and filled up with beer again,' she told me. Immediately, I started to wonder if I could climb over the wall, get some of the empty bottles, take them to *another* pub and get the money back on them again. I talked to my friend, Jimmy Eat, about it and he wasn't sure, but I decided to try taking them to the Off Licence. Sure enough, my plan worked! Every night we could, we climbed over the wall, nicked a few bottles, took them to different Off Licences and made a few coppers.

We also used to walk to Hampstead, which was posh, go into the back gardens and pinch apples, take them home, wash them and make toffee apples. My mother helped us: we bought the sugar and wooden sticks and she made the toffee; we put them on one of her aluminium trays and went round the streets, selling them. Then I'd give my mum the money. We also went round knocking on doors, asking people for rags and then, when we'd got enough, we'd take them to the rag and bone man, get sixpence or a shilling, and I'd give that to Mum too.

We were never short of ideas for making a bit of money. There was army surplus stuff for sale everywhere, and my mum used to buy parachutes for the silk; she made dresses or nighties out of it. I could not have been more than seven or eight when I came up with the idea of Jimmy and I selling them. We went to the army surplus store, and the parachutes were all stacked in the corner; I can still remember the smell of the leather straps. I did the talking while

Jimmy Eat pinched a couple and before long we had sold one to twin boys who lived in the new block of flats at the end of the road. Two days later, there was a bit of a kafuffle when they were spotted standing on the roof of the flats, three stories up, one of them helping the other on with the parachute. Then the one wearing the parachute jumped! He went straight down like a roman candle! It didn't kill him but he broke both his legs, and it was *our fault!* Everybody knew we had been trying to sell them. My dad gave me a good hiding and it goes without saying that we didn't sell any more!

During the war, Dad had been discharged from the army on account of his migraines, and he became an air raid warden, which was worse, he said, because of all the bombing. Ours was a very close-knit community and he told me horrendous stories about how he would be having a cup of tea with somebody one day, only to be picking up their arms and legs the next. It was a terrible time: piles of rubble everywhere, no gas, no water. The community spirit was phenomenal, though, and people got so used to things they had parties to cheer themselves up. They never had any money, but everybody brought something and the local 'wide boy' would always be able to get black-market stuff.

Although I did not do it consciously, I have the feeling that I often did things to make my father feel good about me, which wasn't easy. My dad was into football, and Sam was the footballer in the family, so my dad took more notice of him than Ray or myself. Sam was a brilliant player: he would put milk bottles in the yard and dribble round them and he might have played for Chelsea. They wanted him to try out, but my father said there was no money in football, which there wasn't in those days, and wanted him to learn a trade first.

I joined the Boys' Brigade because he thought it would be good for me. I played the bugle and we walked through the streets every Sunday, after my brothers had made sure all my buttons were shiny and my shoes clean. I can't remember what else we did, and I enjoyed that, but I wasn't a footballer.

I loved boxing, probably because I discovered that it taught me how to handle myself at school. Although I'm only half Jewish, my name was still Moses, and I was a target for bullies. I actually lived the classic situation of one of the worst ones becoming my friend. His name was Tony Davis and he was the ringleader of a group that never left me alone until I completely lost my temper and gave him a good hiding one day. After that, his manner changed – he changed - and not only did he stop picking on me, he didn't pick on anyone else, either.

I carried on with amateur boxing for quite some time because I was good at it. When I was in the ring there was always someone shouting 'Come on! Beat up the Jew boy!' which made me angry and spurred me on. I didn't always win, but I fought that much harder and did my utmost best. To get over the prejudice in those days, Jewish people had to try to be better than everyone else. My trainer, who was one of the McKay brothers – all boxers -, told me to take no notice of them and 'just whack 'em'. So, I did as I was told!

My dad did come to watch me box at school a couple of times, and that made me very proud. I wanted to please him and get closer to him. I do miss him, very much.

On rare occasions, he took off all our doors, including the front door, dismantled the big double bed in their bedroom, and put the lot in the back yard out of the way, giving us enough space inside the house to have a party. All the footballers came, and friends from the street wandered in and out; people brought bottles of beer and we would have a barrel of it to make sure everyone could have a drink; Sam got on the upright piano and there was lots of singing. The next day, Jimmy and I would get our trolleys – special trolleys that Ray had made for me – and collect all the empty bottles to get the money back on them.

My sister, Eileen, had her wedding reception there when I was three. She helped make sandwiches the night before, scrubbed the hall and whitened the front steps the following morning, then got married in the afternoon.

Sam, my eldest brother, was a character. He was very intelligent and started up a school newspaper called *The Spur*, which he wrote and also printed, because the school had some kind of machine, albeit a hand one. It was all before my time (Sam was fourteen years older than me), but, because he was so good at sport, he also had his name up in the assembly hall. It was a big school and there was his name, Samuel Moses! Ray and I were not academic like Sam: we were more mechanical; we could fix things, and we were much more cheeky, so we were in trouble a lot!

Sam hated doing National Service in the army, but they could see something in him too, and were training him for higher things than the usual manoeuvres. I don't know how long he was there, but he hated it so much he pretended to be deaf. They would do things like dropping pennies behind him and try to taunt him by saying 'Here, Jew boy! Pick up the money!' but he would just carry on walking. Eventually, he convinced everybody, including us, that he was deaf, and he was discharged. Funny thing was, by then he *was* deaf! He had been so determined to get out that, to a certain extent, he'd *made* himself deaf and it took quite a while for his hearing to come back.

He and Ray started up a printing business in the washhouse in the back yard. Ray went round with a sample card, knocking on doors to get orders, which he then brought back to Sam, who printed them, one at a time, on a little machine called an Adana. If somebody wanted five hundred, it took a while!

Every day, they cleared up all their stuff so that Mum could do her washing, and, one day, Jimmy Eat and I were playing in there because Mum had the copper going and it was lovely and warm. There were several cracks in the concrete oven, and she had often asked my dad to fix them because all the heat was escaping, but he never had. I got a pot of black ink and poked that into the cracks, none too neatly but thinking I was doing Mum a favour. The ink was quite thick but because the concrete was so hot it soon formed a skin, looked like it was dry, and I thought we'd done it. An hour or two later, I heard my mum screaming and yelling: she had taken her washing out and got black ink all over everything!

The calamities were not yet over that day, however. I was not feeling well and I had gone to bed. Jimmy was still with me and he said he was freezing. I told him Mum would not light the fires until later, so he went and got some wood and lit one on the lino floor of the bedroom! Mum smelled burning and when Jimmy heard her coming he kicked all the burning wood under the bed. We were kids: what did we know?! The mattress was straw and it caught fire. It was a nightmare! Mum put it out, but did I get a larruping from my dad!

Not long after that, my dad won a hundred pounds on the football pools, which was a *lot* of money then. He helped Sam and Ray buy their first professional printing machine and they set up their business in a former sweet shop across the road. The bookie's runner would sometimes run in there to hide. (Betting was illegal at the time, and the runners would be on street corners taking bets for the bookies.) The police always knew where our local one was. They would make a lot of noise coming along the street, because they had to be seen to be doing their job. Invariably, though, they were betting with him as well.

Sam and Ray were immensely proud of their printing machine, despite the fact that it was second or third hand, very old and in poor shape. Every time it broke down, Ray would simply patch it up with tape and a length of string. He had previously worked for an engineering firm, and he was very good at thinking logically and analytically, working out the mechanics of any machine and repairing it when it broke down.

On many occasions they would ask me to look after it when they went out with their girlfriends. I was only eight or nine at the time and loved the feeling that they were giving me trust and responsibility. The printer had a number box, indicating how many sheets of paper it had printed, and, before they left, they started it running; then I was responsible for shutting it down when it reached the specific number of sheets to be printed, and for ringing my mum and dad to tell them. The telephone had no dialling facility: I had to generate the signal by turning the handle several times and it would then ring at our house. Very few families in Kilburn had a telephone, but we needed one for the business.

It was during this time that I first became interested in art, although I did not recognise it as such. While the printer was running, and I had nothing to do, I would go into the small room at the back of the shop and settle down to paint myself a masterpiece with different coloured inks. I can still smell the aroma as I mixed different colours on white card, which seemed to come very naturally to me, and seeing the bright colours blending into each other was something I found exciting.

There was little opportunity to explore that interest, of course. Art was not considered a serious subject in a place like Kilburn and although I always got good school reports in art, no one ever encouraged me. There would have been no point in asking my dad if I could go to Art College, anyway. We were living in deepest London, and everybody needed money to live and eat. I would have got some very strange looks all round if it had become known that I wanted to be an artist.

For the same reason, I had no opportunity to indulge my growing love of clothes. My mother did once buy me a tan leather jacket, though. Whether or not it was real leather, I don't know, and how she got the money, I haven't got a clue. To go with it, she bought me a tie with sword-fighting pirates on it, as I remember. On my first day of wearing the jacket, I happened to open the door to a man who said he was a photographer and asked if my mother was there. Ray was home on leave from National Service, at the time, and liked the idea of a photo of me, so he said he would pay for it - ten shillings - in instalments. Of course, he went back to the army and my mother had to pay it off.

Nevertheless, it was just as well we got a picture as I only had the jacket for a few days. Although it was the 1950's, parts of London were still devastated and we used to play on the bombsites: we climbed up onto the rafters of the bombed buildings opposite our house, walked along them and threw asbestos (imagine!) plaster at each other because when it hit the floor, it exploded like a bomb; it was good for war games. I was on top of the rafters as usual, this day, showing off in my new jacket, and fell off. As luck would have it, there were nails sticking out of the wooden planks; I got caught by one ripping into the jacket, and I was left hanging while Jim went running for our other mates to help him get me down. But then I had to go home and tell my mother what had happened. I'll never forget it: she cried, which made me cry, and she said, 'I'm only crying because I know what's going to happen to you when Dad gets home.' And it did!

Although art was so far out of the question that no one even thought about it, including me, I also liked the idea of taking pictures and when I got my first camera, which was an old Kodak Brownie that my parents got from somewhere, I carried it with me whenever I could. Even though we could rarely afford to get the films processed, and I wouldn't have had the words to explain it then, I loved taking pictures because I began to discover the art in photography and what really makes a picture.

We were poor, and it was rough, but I thought it was all a lovely life. We had no aspirations or expectations, we never stole off our own and if we got our 'grub', that was enough. From the start, contributing whatever I could came naturally to me; it was part of the air I breathed, not because my parents asked me to or expected anything – they never did – but because it was in me. I automatically looked for ways to help my family, even in school: a couple of the mini-bottles of school milk went home to my mum whenever I could manage it. It was a game – a kind of play, if you like – arising out of an innate ability to survive, or maybe kick-starting it.

For my parents though, it was hard labour. When I was about seven, I remember seeing my mother crying and desperate because we had no money. Without her knowing, I raided the gas meter and gave her the money. It took me ages to work out how to do it and then fix the lock back on again, but I managed it and made up some lie so that she never knew where the money came from. I should probably not admit to that, but in that area and with what we had to live on, if people didn't do anything at all they wouldn't have survived.

When Eileen and Sam were little, my mum regularly put them both in the pram and walked miles so that no one would see her pawning my father's overcoat. When he got paid, she walked all the way back to redeem it. What could you get for an overcoat?! Enough food for a few days, maybe. For years, she said she had lost her engagement ring, but she had pawned it and never been able to get it back. There were no benefits like Income Support then. The Welfare State started in 1948, but everything was means tested: someone would come into your house and put a value on your furniture, or whatever you had, and expect you to sell it before any help was given. It was degrading. For most people, if they didn't have money, they didn't eat, and that was all there was to it.

Despite all that, our road was a community and we all helped each other. Mum only bought food day to day to make sure she had enough money, and then she would cook for everybody, including my nan at the end of the road and the poor, mad, war veteran who lived upstairs. He had been gassed in the First World War and was slightly deranged. The smell of candles still reminds me of him because he did not have electricity, or could not afford to use it, and he always lit candles. He had matches all the way along the ledge beside the gas mantle in his room, and there was always the pungent, mixed smell of sulphur and wax. The wax didn't bother me but, to this day, I hate the smell of sulphur and the feel of matches: they make me nauseous, and if I touch a match I have to wash my hands.

One of us was looking out of our window one day, and spotted him climbing out of his window, trying to get onto the telephone lines. We all went up and dragged him back in. That man had fought in the war, won medals, lost part of a toe, been gassed, his wife had died, and this country had left him to rot. Nobody was looking after him, so my mother used to give me a plate of food to take up to him and a plate to take all the way up to my nan. Then I would go back for the empty plates and make sure they were all right.

My mother had nothing but she coped with everything, and if she ever had any spare cash she would buy a small bag of sweets and let us have two a day. She was a fantastic woman. I wish I had talked to her more and asked her about different things, but I didn't. You don't think about it until it's too late.

# 2

# A Good Idea at the Time

I was thirteen when my dad changed the name Moses. Within our community, where everyone knew us, there was no prejudice against Jews. Outside it, however, it was common. My dad changed it when we were finally moving into a council house because he thought no one would know us in the new place. As it turned out, everyone in the street was moved to Stonebridge, the same as us! I do believe he also changed it to help my brothers' business.

Janet had been working in Boston as a nanny for a family called Grayson, and she wanted to change to that name. I didn't have a choice.

With a new name and a new house came a new beginning. As soon as we moved, Jimmy Eat and I decided we would start up a building business. We didn't have any experience but we didn't let that bother us. Sam and Ray printed some leaflets and cards for us and we duly posted these through letterboxes, obviously not around where we lived but on the outskirts. A few weeks went by and we heard nothing - not one call, not one enquiry. Then, in the August just before my fourteenth birthday, we had a call from a local dentist.

Mr McCabe explained that he was having problems with his drill and asked if we had any

23

experience in this type of work. I assured him that we had, and Jimmy and I arranged to go round to his surgery the next day. We were very excited about getting our first job, although Jimmy was also very nervous. For some reason, I wasn't: I was confident that we could do the job and do it well.

We arrived at the surgery on time and were shown into the waiting room by Mrs McCabe; she told us that Mr McCabe would not be long. It looked nice enough: the walls were a brilliant white; the furniture and woodwork were black; and the windows had the posh lead glazing that my mum would have loved. Mr McCabe came in after a couple of minutes and apologised for keeping us waiting. I introduced myself and Jimmy.

'You two look a bit young to be doing this kind of work,' said Mr McCabe.

'Yes I know,' I replied, 'but my family has been in the trade for years and they've shown me everything they know. We've worked in a few dentists' surgeries before, so you don't need to worry.'

Mr McCabe proceeded to show us what was wrong with the chair and drill, which were connected: the water was not getting through to the drill bit. After looking at it, I told him that fixing it would not be a problem and he seemed very pleased. He told us that he was hoping to get the ceiling painted later on in the week and wanted it all finished as soon as possible so that he could re-open his surgery.

'Why don't you let us paint the ceiling for you?' I piped up, thinking only of the money we would get.

'Can you do it?' Mr McCabe asked, sounding hopeful.

'Of course we can,' I said. 'Jim's dad is a decorator. There isn't much he doesn't know, and Jim has worked with him.

'Right, Jim?' I added, warming to my theme.

Jim agreed although he looked very anxious. Mr McCabe looked at us thoughtfully, but then said he would get the paint while we fixed the chair.

After he left, Jim looked fit to burst. 'Christ Steve! What are we going to do?' he snapped.

'It can't be that difficult,' I smiled.

Neither of us had a clue what we were doing, but we did it anyway. I got a screwdriver out of my bag and started to take the side off the chair to uncover the mechanics. Bloody hell! I thought. I had never seen so many wires, and other things I didn't even know the name of, in all my young life. We both started to panic then, and it was a good thing the dentist didn't see our faces at this stage. I carried on regardless and noticed all these very small plastic pipes running through the chair, which carried the water up to the drill bit. 'I think all we need is something to clean these pipes out,' I said hopefully. 'Go and get some pipe cleaners from that shop over the road.'

Jim's shoulders seemed to sag. He was not at all sure about messing around with the innards of the chair but, bless him, he went to the shop anyway and came back with four packets of pipe cleaners.

I twisted about a dozen of them together and pushed them down through the pipes. Sure enough, all the green fungus that was stuck in the plastic piping seemed to disappear. Fantastic! We put all the parts back, praying that they were in the right places, and then fixed the cover back onto the chair. Just as I was replacing the last screw, Mr McCabe arrived back with two large tins of paint.

'Have you started on the chair yet?' he asked, looking around.

'We've finished,' I announced.

'That was quick! Is it working all right now?'

Jim and I nodded and then looked at each other anxiously as he proceeded to walk over to the chair and pick up the drill to test it. He switched it on and out came water. I couldn't believe that we had done it!

'How much do I owe you?' he asked, really pleased.

'Don't worry!' I said. 'We still have to paint the ceiling. We'll do it now, if you like, and you can pay us when we're finished.'

'Very well,' he agreed. 'There's a ladder in the back and I'm sure you'll find everything you need in the way of brushes in the shed.'

He showed us the way to the back door and left us to get on with the rest of the job, apparently assured that we were as good as our word and knew exactly what we were doing.

Outside, there was an old set of ladders propped up against the wall. Jimmy examined them. 'We can't use these; they're crap,' he decided.

'They'll be fine, Jim, stop your whining,' I called from the shed, rummaging in a box of old brushes and pulling out two that looked all right. I found a stick to mix the paint and we took it all back inside.

'I think we should put something on the floor to catch the drips,' said Jimmy as I mixed the paint.

'Let's just get on with it!' I said impatiently.

As I mounted the first step on the ladder there was a creak. I carried on, clenching my teeth, determined to get this done. When I got to the top, Jimmy held the ladder steady while I painted. I was getting on all right – not too much paint on the brush, no drips - until the step I was standing on gave way. The paint can flew out of my hand as I instinctively reached out to grab something and fell. I landed on my back, winded, and struggled to my feet to look at the damage. The dentist's chair and the beautiful black and white tiled floor were splattered with thick, white, gloopy paint.

'Fuck, Jim! What are we going to do?' I gasped.

I remembered having seen my dad painting and cleaning up any spillages with white spirit. We managed to find some out in the shed, along with what looked like old rags in a basket by the door, and we cleaned everything as best we could. The surgery was full of fumes and stunk, but there was nothing we could do about that. We finished the ceiling as quickly as we could. It looked a bit patchy, but we had had enough by this time and sneaked out without seeing the dentist, feeling very relieved to be out of there; we did not have the nerve to ask for what he owed us.

We heard nothing from him for a couple of days, which I thought was a good thing. But good things never last! I got home on the third day and Mum shouted from the kitchen that there had been a phone call for me from a Mr McCabe, saying he wanted to see me and Jimmy straight away. I went and got Jimmy and we jogged round to his house. Well, what can I say? He opened the front door and just started yelling, calling us a pair of idiots, saying that while he had been using the drill on a patient the water had suddenly stopped and the patient's tooth had been burnt and cracked. He had had to get someone in to sort it all out as well as placate a very irate patient. Apparently, I hadn't actually cleaned the pipes. I had just dislodged the fungus and rearranged it so that it eventually settled at the base of the mechanism.

'Does that mean you're not going to pay us?' I asked, jokingly. 'We did paint the ceiling.'

Mr McCabe did not see the funny side: he went bright red and I thought he might explode. 'You left the place stinking!' he yelled. '*And* the cloths you used to clear up after yourselves were tea towels my wife had just taken off the washing line. So, *no*! I am *not* paying you! And if you show your faces here again you'll have to pay me not to kill the pair of you! Now clear off!'

Well, you have to start somewhere, even if it is at the wrong end! We carried on with our business, not letting that one mistake make a difference. We got better at it and managed to get quite a lot of work.

On one occasion we were asked to do a roofing job. Obviously, we had never done one before but, again, that did not bother us in the least. The problem was we didn't have a ladder. We tried to borrow one, but nobody had one long enough, so we thought we would try and buy a new one on hire purchase. We bought a copy of *Exchange and Mart* and rushed back to our 'office', which was either Jimmy's bedroom or mine, depending on which one we were in at the time. Jimmy filled out the application form with our 'company' name and we sent off for our first piece of equipment - a twenty foot ladder.

I remember the day it arrived. It was a fantastic wooden ladder with red runners. My mum went mad because she had to pay the first instalment, although she didn't know it was an instalment! She would have hit the roof if she had known we got it on hire purchase, which started after the war and got a lot of people into debt and financial difficulty. My dad never got to know about the ladder, let alone the hire purchase! And we never did pay anymore after the first instalment. We got demanding letters, which Jimmy took care of, but I can't remember how. I think he disbanded the company!

Fortunately, the roofing job fell through at the last minute; it could have been a disaster if we had mucked that one up. And although we had the ladder, we never did much with it because we had no transport and had to carry it to wherever the work was. We soon sold it, making a profit, of course, and I paid back the instalment to my mum.

Our main problem was that we did not have enough money to buy materials, so we had to ask the clients for money up front. Since there was no guarantee they would ever see us or their money again, most of them refused.

Thus, my first business came to an end

# 3
# Out Into the World

My father, who was quite clever, always said you should have a basic education but the main thing was earning money, so I left school at fourteen with a crappy education, which was probably nobody's fault but my own.

Looking back, I wish I'd studied more, but they didn't have much time for me and there was a lot of stuff I didn't learn. The headmaster used to say, while hitting me round the head, that I would rather make people laugh than do any work. I did lark about a lot and as long as I was doing that I thought bugger the rest! I hated school. I did like metal work, but even then I mucked about. I pretended to throw a metal file at the teacher's back when he was walking by one time. The file, which was fitted into a wooden handle, must have been a bit loose because it left the handle and flew past his ear. I had not meant that to happen and I was horrified. He stopped, turned round and without saying a word picked up a big metal ruler and threw it at me, which could have done me a lot of damage. Fortunately, his aim was no good and it missed me. He then sat down, wrote a letter, handed it to me and told me to make sure my father got it. Of course he never did!

I'm dyslexic, but dyslexia was unheard of then. I had to go to a special school once a week. It wasn't only me – we went in a coach and lots of kids were picked up – but I felt weird about it because I was the only one from my school. They did a good job though. I had difficulty pronouncing words (I still do - I know the word but I cannot say it) and they gave me help with that, and with distinguishing numbers, which I got confused. I also learned to read and write, but writing was always more of a challenge. I could write something like 'steel magnolias' but I could not write 'in' or 'at'. They would ask why I wrote the long words and not the short ones, and I would tell them that I could not write them because I did not know what they were. The word 'this': I couldn't say it, couldn't write it. My brain could not get round the small words and the teachers just thought I was round the twist.

I still have those problems. My dyslexia is getting worse with age. Printed words start to move around, especially when I concentrate for too long. I have to take my eyes off the page for a minute and then go back. If that happens too much, I get a pain over my eye and a migraine that might last up to three days. So, even though I love reading about all kinds of different things, it's difficult and takes me a long time because of the constant stopping. Other times, I'll be reading something and suddenly I come to a word that, for no apparent reason, I can't read: my mind goes blank. I might be typing and that will happen, so I leave those words out until they come back to me. And they're *always* small words. Sometimes I get letters jumbled up: 'I' and 'l' in the same word, like 'girl', confuse me; I don't know where to put them. After I've typed it, I can see if I've done it wrong and then I correct it because I know how it should be spelled.

It's ironic that I'm a journalist because, of course, I have to write stories. Fortunately, they then go to a sub editor who polishes them up.

Underneath all the playacting at school, I'm sure I did want to learn because I've never stopped learning since. I can't get enough. I can't get enough of everything!

A couple of weeks before leaving school, we had to go for an interview with the careers officer. When he asked me what I wanted to do, I said art or printing. He told me there was no way I'd get into art college, and I wasn't educated enough to be a printer. He seemed to think that I was best suited to the army. Both my brothers had done their National Service in the army and they had told me all about it, so I knew it wasn't all good, but I was not deterred and went home to talk to my parents about it. Naturally, my mum was dead set against it, but not my dad. 'It'll do him good, Min,' he said, and I arranged to go to the recruiting centre the next day.

'I'm coming with you,' said Mum with tears in her eyes.

'No you're not!' said Dad. 'Ray can go with him.'

It was a beautiful sunny morning and looking in the window of the recruiting office I could see pictures of soldiers in bearskin hats and red and gold uniforms standing outside Buckingham Palace. That's me! I thought.

When we went in, there were quite a few people in the office already being interviewed, but an officer soon called us over. He seemed a nice enough fellow and asked me if I had come to join up.

'Yes, Sir,' I replied respectfully.

'I suppose you want to stand outside Buckingham Palace, don't you?'

'Yes, Sir.'

The officer carried on about how good the army was, and how you get to travel around the world for free. I could see my brother was getting slightly irritated, to say the least. He knew what it was really like.

'The first thing we'll teach you is how to dress and be clean,' said the officer, with a sudden change in attitude. 'I can't believe your mother let you out of the house in those ridiculous trousers.'

'They're modern, Sir,' I explained.

'Modern?' he said. 'If you think you'll be wearing them in the army, you'll be disappointed, lad!'

That was it! Ray had heard enough and dragged me out of the office. I was really annoyed with him, but when Mum heard that the soldier had criticised my trousers, she agreed with Ray. Apart from that, she was overjoyed that I hadn't joined up. My dad, on the other hand, had a different opinion. 'It would have done him good,' he said, always a man of few words.

I went to work for my brothers. They had moved their printing business a couple of miles away, to Swiss Cottage, when developers had taken over the old place to demolish it and build a block of high-rise flats on the land.

It was my first proper job, and I gave my mum ten shillings a week. I found out later that she always saved half a crown of that to buy me clothes, bless her. I was a general dog's body, running around, making tea and watching the printers. When I was fifteen, a couple of months after I started, my brothers decided to send me to North Western Polytechnic, on day release. I was terrified of going back to school again: I had visions of not being able to learn anything.

I went every Monday, and the first one was dark and cold, with the skies threatening to open any minute. Just before I got to the college, they did, and I got absolutely soaked; I had water dripping off every part of me. I went into a huge room with green pillars, which to me at that age was very intimidating, and waited until they called my name. Shivering and dripping water, I hurried forward to sign my name in a large leather-bound book. The man behind the desk told me to go and dry off in the toilets.

While I was trying to do that with paper towels, I realized that my life was about to change: I had become a grown-up; I was on my own now, and I had to do well for my brothers. I began singing one of the latest songs, *I want to be Bobby's Girl*. I sang louder, enjoying the echo around me and not realising that I was not alone: there was another boy in one of the cubicles.

'Hi!' he said with a smirk as he emerged. 'So you want to be Bobby's girl, do you?'

I had never really known anyone who was homosexual, so I didn't catch the innuendo. I just chatted to him for a minute about it being my first day, and then made my way to a large classroom filled with about five printing machines. The teacher grouped us in threes and then climbed onto a chair and started showing us various parts of the machines.

After about an hour I felt really good: I was finally enjoying being taught, and I was learning to do things the right way. Apart from schoolwork, I had always thought I could do anything, because I did seem to pick things up very quickly: jack-of-all-trades, master of none - that was me. But I had never had formal training in anything. I was especially determined to get this right and show my brothers, who meant the world to me, that they were justified in trusting me with this opportunity.

The time flew by and before I knew it, it was time for lunch. The canteen was very old-fashioned: there were giant metal pillars and metal girders spanning the entire ceiling. I was feeling confident by this time: me, at college, who'd have thought it? I wondered if my mum and dad were proud of me. I knew my mum would be, but I could not ever remember having a conversation with my dad for more than a couple of minutes. I was wishing he had shown more interest in me.

Lost in my thoughts, I had forgotten where I was until I looked up from my sandwich and caught sight of the guy who had been in the toilets. 'Hi there!' I called. 'I'm sorry, I can't remember your name.'

'I'm Tony,' he said, shaking my hand. He sat down opposite me while I tucked into the rest of my lunch. 'Who do you work for?' he asked.

'My brothers. They own a business in Swiss Cottage and they sent me here to learn the trade. I don't know if I like it yet, but they want me to go into the family business.'

I was fifteen; Tony was two years older. It was 1962, and the Beatles were top of the hit parade. Tony mentioned to me that he liked all pop music, and that one of his friends was in the pop business. 'Brian Epstein,' he said. I wasn't that impressed because I didn't know who he was talking about, but when I heard, 'manager of the Beatles', I nearly choked on my lunch.

When I was fourteen and still at school in Paddington, I had started going out with a lovely girl called Barbara, whom I met in the schoolyard. She was my first girlfriend, the usual teenage infatuation and very innocent because, in those days, teenage girls were not generally as sexually active as they are now. I really liked her so I respected that and didn't try anything. When we first got to know each other, we were sitting on a bench on Paddington recreation ground, one day, just talking. I can still see it: the lovely little gardens and the swings; me, wondering how to get off with her. I don't know where I got the idea, but I pointed to a blackbird in a tree and when she looked up I kissed her. I suppose I didn't want to do it with her looking at me! She went all coy and seemed to like it, but she had been brought up to be a 'good girl'. Her parents were very straight laced, and she'd been taught that anything more than a kiss was reserved for marriage. One evening, we went back to her house when her parents were out. I had high hopes for that evening! And we might have got further than a kiss, but I'll never know because a friend from school knocked on the door and put a stop to anything.

I was still going out with her when I met Tony. I had asked him if he had a girlfriend and he said he didn't, which I found strange because he was very good looking. I still did not realize he was gay and he didn't tell me because, back then, no one advertised the fact. After two or three weeks at college, I asked him if he would like to go out with Barbara and me, and he agreed. He was very well spoken and Barbara was greatly impressed. I got a little annoyed, thinking she fancied him, but that could not have been further from the truth. Once he had left and I questioned her about her feelings, she told me straight, 'Tony's gay!' *She* had been worried that he fancied *me!* I felt cold at the thought.

A couple of days later, Tony invited me to a party. I have to say, I was a bit worried after what Barbara had said, plus the fact that he hadn't invited her to the party. I decided I would just have to make it very clear to him that I was straight, if he was in any doubt after meeting Barbara.

I will never forget that Saturday evening. The doorbell rang and my mum opened the door. 'Stephen, it's your friend,' she shouted up the stairs. When I came down and saw him in his flared trousers and flowery shirt I nearly passed out. He also smelt like he had just come from a perfume factory. I just hoped that Dad wouldn't see him, or smell him.

'Are you ready Steve?' he said.

Shit! Ready for what? I thought.

There were two other boys in the back of an open top MG, which was 'the business' in those days.

I climbed in the front and looked round to see if my mum and dad were watching from the doorstep, but fortunately my dad wasn't there, just Mum waving and shouting ''bye boys'. I was so embarrassed because the two boys in the back were waving back. There we were, driving through a tough council estate, camping it up! I would never be able to show my face in Stonebridge Park again.

Tony casually said we were going to St Johns Wood to see a friend of his. I thought nothing of it until I saw the house. What an amazing house it was! Five storeys of complete luxury! I had never seen anything like it in my life, let alone been in one! 'Is it flats?' I asked in awe.

'I don't think so, love!' Tony laughed. That was the first time I had heard him say anything camp. I didn't like it and was even more worried about his motives. I should have left then, but curiosity got the better of me.

Tony rang the doorbell and a short, portly man, dressed in striped trousers and a black jacket, opened the door. 'Come in, Master Tony,' he said.

*What's that all about?!* I thought.

The inside of the house was more magnificent than the outside. There was antique furniture everywhere, and gold leaf columns surrounded a spiral wooden staircase. The woodwork was all so shiny I could see my face in it.

'Welcome!' a voice echoed down the staircase. 'Who's this Tony?' asked the man coming into view.

'This is Steve,' said Tony.

'Ah, the boy you met at college,' he said, turning to me. 'I'm Harry.'

'Pleased to meet you,' I said, shaking his hand.

We followed him into a large living room and the butler brought in a tray of drinks. We sat and got comfortable.

'I've invited a few friends over for drinks and I'm glad you could join us,' said Harry.

I sat there, feeling perplexed, wondering what we were doing there.

'Do you enjoy printing, Steve?' he asked.

'Yes, I work with my brothers,' I replied stiffly. 'What do you do?'

He and Tony looked at each other in amazement while I just sat there looking like a fool. You could have heard a pin drop.

'Don't you recognize him?' Tony finally asked with a grin.

'Should I?' I was getting embarrassed as their eyes stayed on me.

'Young man, I'm in management, mainly in the music business,' Harry explained.

I stammered an apology, now completely tongue-tied, and was thankful when Tony asked who else was coming and took the attention off me.

An hour passed and the room filled with people, even some women, which cheered me up a lot. I thought I might have seen a couple of the men on television, but I couldn't put names to faces. Tony introduced me to Billy Fury and after talking to him for a while I figured that he was of the same persuasion as Tony. He was a nice guy and certainly knew Tony very well. I talked to many celebrities that evening. The one who impressed me the most was Cliff Richard: he was talking to two girls for most of the time.

I overheard two men having a conversation about Abbey Road Studios and I knew that was where the Beatles recorded. I was very fond of Beatles music and so was Jimmy. I wasn't going to let an opportunity like this go by, so, not being backward in coming forward, I decided to chat to these two men. 'Hi! Nice to meet you. I'm a friend of Billy's,' I said, thinking, *well I am now.* To this day I cannot understand why these people gave me the time of day, but they did. I let them do most of the talking and found out that one of them was a sound engineer at Abbey Road and the other was a producer. They were surprised that I had never been to the studios, seeing as I was so friendly with Billy, but I managed to bullshit my way out of that one.

We left there at about eleven and Tony suggested going to a club in Soho. They were obviously loaded, which I wasn't, so I told him that I didn't have the money. He just laughed it off, said it didn't matter and that I didn't need to worry about money; he just wanted us to enjoy ourselves.

Over the next few months, I went out with Tony and his friends all the time, and at no time did we discuss that he was homosexual. By that time I didn't care; he was a great guy and he knew I was straight. Barbara met him a few times, but she didn't have the connection with him that I had.

One night he took me to the Vauxhall Tavern, a very large pub with a bar that encircled the whole of the interior. When we arrived it was heaving, and the air was full of the smell of aftershave. There was only a scattering of women and I decided that this was definitely a gay bar. Tony told me to relax and said that I would really enjoy myself. The music started up and the lights dimmed; everybody clapped and shouted; a spotlight lit up a curtain next to the bar, and out came a six-foot transvestite, introduced as 'Dorothy'. 'Her' legs were so long they seemed to reach to 'her' neck, and 'she' started to sing *Yellow Brick Road* from *The Wizard of Oz*. It was one of the best shows I had ever seen, and we had a great evening.

Finally, the day came when I walked through the doors of Abbey Road Studios with Tony. I was so excited just to be walking through the same doors as some really famous people that I didn't notice how boring it actually looked inside. To the right, there was a reception area with two girls at a switchboard; to the left, there were some tables and chairs where people were sitting around having coffee. It all looked pretty exciting to me.

We were ushered into a large room with pictures of the latest pop stars; I can remember the smell of fresh coffee and cigarettes. Tony's friend - the sound engineer - turned up and said, 'Hi Steve, it's nice to see you again. Would you like some lunch before we go into the recording studio?' I couldn't believe that he had remembered my name, but I quickly agreed. A small staircase led us down to the canteen area. I was not impressed with the decoration: I thought it could do with some renovating. It was just like any other canteen: four or five people behind the counter and a load of people queuing for food. When I joined the end of the queue, I couldn't believe the people I suddenly recognised in front of me: John Lennon, Paul McCartney, George Harrison, and Gene Pitney. I stood with my mouth open in complete shock, but Tony didn't take any notice of them.

'There are three of the Beatles in this queue!' I said, nudging him.

'Yes. They do record here you know?' he smiled.

We got our food and sat down to eat, but I couldn't stop my eyes wandering over to where the three Beatles sat. Once lunch was finished, we were shown to Studio Two by the sound engineer and we stood with him behind the sound controls, which he began operating. As we stood around chatting and I was asking questions about the different buttons on the control panels, the four arrived: John, Paul, George and Ringo. I became absolutely speechless. They were laughing and joking, waving at us through the glass as they made their way to the microphones. Then the music started. It was fantastic, although every now and then John and Paul started giggling uncontrollably, which greatly upset the sound engineer. Who cared, though? These were the Beatles! The session lasted for three hours that seemed like one. I was star struck: mesmerized by the Beatles and engrossed in the music and lyrics. They left the studio, waving and shouting through the glass, 'See you in the bar, guys!'

As we entered the packed bar area, the sound engineer took us over to where the Beatles were standing and introduced me. They all seemed like nice guys. Tony started acting very camp, which annoyed me, but the boys didn't seem to care. Looking around me, I could see there were a lot of fellows in there of the same persuasion. I thought it must be quite prevalent in this kind of business.

I was still going out with Barbara, but not for much longer. I've still got a CD of a record she bought me: Dave Brubeck, *Countdown: Time in Outer Space,* which came out in 1962, after the Russians had launched the first manned space flight in 1961. When she gave it to me, it was Christmas; we exchanged gifts on Clifton Hill in St John's Wood, surrounded by snow. You don't forget your first love and I'll never forget Barbara. But then in 1963, I met Maureen.

# 4
# Show Biz and Plumbing Cocktail

I had been working for my brothers at Swiss Cottage for a while when one particular freezing, snowy day we had a burst pipe. Sam rang our cousin Dennis, who was a plumber, and he came straight away. I was fascinated, watching him turn the water off, unfreeze the pipes and get the water back on. I really liked the look of plumbing and over the coming months I thought hard about the work I had seen Dennis doing. Finally, I spoke to my brothers about it; they were a little taken aback but both agreed that they would not mind me going to learn plumbing. They assured me there would always be a job for me with them if it didn't work out.

I remembered Tony saying he knew a builder, so I rang him and asked him to get me an interview. Sure enough, I got my interview with a man named George. The minute I walked into his office he said 'If you think you are going to get an easy ride, you've got another think coming.' He gave me an address in Stanmore, Middlesex, and told me to be there for 7am the next day. When I got home, Ray looked up the address for me and told me it would take two buses to get there. I would have to leave at 6am.

After getting up at 5am and shovelling some breakfast down my throat, I went out into the freezing cold, eventually getting to the building site with five minutes to spare and feeling a bit anxious about what to expect. Little did I know what was waiting for me.

'Where's George?' I asked a couple of blokes.

'George who?' they said.

'George, the plumber,' I said.

'He doesn't get in until 7.30,' one of them said.

I was mightily pissed off at having to get up so early when George knew I didn't have to be there for another half hour. Nevertheless, I decided to make the most of the time and have a cup of tea to warm me up. There were lots of men queuing up outside a structure made out of scaffolding with a tarpaulin over the top, and I thought that must be the canteen. Wrong! It was the toilet, which I also needed after my long and cold journey, so I queued with the rest of the blokes. When it was my turn, I wished I hadn't bothered. I couldn't believe what I saw: there were about seven 'navvies' sitting in a line on a wooden plank over a massive great hole in the ground, all reading newspapers. The smell was indescribable.

'Come on, son, there's room over here,' said one of the men.

'No thanks,' I said.

That smell will stay with me for the rest of my life!

It was a hard life on a building site in those days: 6am until 6pm, and half an hour for lunch; there was no Portaloo, no proper canteen, and you had to conform – or else!

I hated the plumber foreman, who clouted me round the head if I did something wrong. There was also an 'initiation' I had to go through after I'd done my first house - put all the pipes in and so on. I was told I would just be dunked in a tank of water, so when they grabbed hold of me I thought that was what they were going to do. They laid me on the ground, and I stayed there because I thought everyone went through this; they put three half hundredweight sacks of cement on my torso and legs so that I couldn't move; they held my arms, got my dick out and put fine grains of sand up the opening. It hurt, but then the pain stopped, until I went to pee and the sand scraped the urethra as it came down; *then* the pain was unbelievable. For a week or so I was in agony. I did not go to the doctor or make a complaint; my dad said to just leave it because if I made a fuss I'd never be accepted. And that's what happened: I was treated as part of the team after that.

I still hated the foreman though; he continued to be horrible, so I found ways to get my own back. I had to make the tea and wash the cups with water and sand – rubbing the sand all round the inside of each cup. I would leave grains of sand in the foreman's tea. He drank it and never noticed so I decided to go one step further: I put in a bit of Yorkshire flux (used for soldering) and it melted instantly. It made the tea look greasy but I gave it to him anyway. He drank it and didn't even taste anything different. I did it everyday, hoping he would get 'the runs'. He never did!

After about two years of being an apprentice I knew quite a lot about plumbing and even more about life.

I know the men did things to me that would be called abuse now, and they shouldn't have. But I survived it. It was good life experience because it taught me respect, and if I could survive that I could do *anything*! I wasn't afraid of much after that, and I didn't care about inhibitions: I couldn't give a monkey's!

After George and the other plumbers on site had taught me all there was to know about 'first fixing', which means putting all the main pipes in the house, bar the fittings, I decided I knew enough to go out on my own; I did not want to be a plumber's mate anymore. I looked in all the evening papers to find a job, and I did not listen to anyone who said 'don't run before you can walk'. My philosophy all through my life has been, if you don't ask you don't get. It is the only way I have been able to survive and bounce back from hardship to make things better than before. Experience has taught me that you can do anything if you have the right frame of mind.

Eventually, I managed to get a job with a company in St Martins Lane, right in the heart of London. It was a well-established building company that had been around for about sixty years, although it looked very old-fashioned to me. They suggested that I go out with another plumber for the first few times to get a little experience, and I must say I was pleased about that because I was a little worried about coping on my own. Although, if I'd had to, I would have, because that was me all over - in feet first.

The company's primary source of business was the maintenance and emergency plumbing needs of the major companies in the area, and I learnt the filthy end of the business very quickly. Fred was the guy who first trained me on the job and he took me down into the sewers. There were no masks or protective clothing in those days, and we would go about ten feet below street level under Covent Garden and walk all the way to Trafalgar Square in the sewer; it was not pleasant. There were walkways along the sides, the water flowing in between. I never saw a live rat, because they were scared of us, but I could continually hear the plop of them jumping into the water. I saw a dead one floating, once, and it's true that they're as big as cats. It had a twizzly tail and I still shudder whenever I see something that shape. There were giant, mesh-covered holes at intervals along the walls and these serviced about a hundred houses each. As we came to one, Fred would shout for me to stop if he heard the rush of water, sewage and everything else coming down. Like I said, it was not pleasant – a load of shit, in fact!

Later, I went out with an Irishman named Ron, who was a very agreeable fellow but a bit of a joker. He pushed me in front of one of these holes and I got clobbered with the full force of crap coming out. Fred went mad because the force could have thrown me into the main channel and I could, literally, have drowned in shit! Not to mention the danger of disease.

It did not end there with Ron. One of the regular monthly jobs at all the pubs was cleaning out traps or interceptors, which were filters to stop all the rats and rubbish coming in. The main one for each pub was in the sewer, accessed through the basement, and, because I was young and new, I got the job of going down there. The first time I went down, I was ladling all the goo into a container when I heard the sound of something being shifted across the floor above, and the light was going. I looked up and saw Ron pushing the cover back on. Before I had time to do anything, the cover fell into place and I was in absolute darkness. I didn't think about the fact that the cover was cast iron and it had taken the two of us to get it off. I just thought he would open it again in a minute and I leant against the wall to wait, forgetting about the white jelly-like slime that covered the walls of all the sewers. I thought it was grease, anyway; it looked like white grease and I had never touched it. The smell was horrendous, of course; then I felt this slime on my back, which disgusted me and I jerked away, but it had gone through my overall and was irritating my skin.

Ron seemed to take forever to lift the cover. Of course, he'd had to find somebody to help him lift it off. Eventually, the cover came off, light flooded in, and they were all there, peering down and laughing at me. Men are *so* stupid! I climbed the steps and got out, and they told me to go and look at myself in the mirror. I couldn't believe what I saw, but I understood why my skin was irritated. I was covered in some kind of lice or maggoty things! This stuff on the walls was alive! I wasn't squeamish about most things, but I could not get my clothes off and myself into the shower fast enough.

The company also did maintenance for Charing Cross Hospital (now a police station). The first time I went there was with Ron, and when I asked what we had to do he just said that I probably wouldn't like it but I would get used to it. It was an enormous, old-fashioned building smelling of chloroform. The first job of the day was more dirty work: cleaning out the drains and the sinks with a foul smelling liquid called *Blue Devil*. It was acid, and as soon as water was added to it a chemical reaction occurred, which made anything that came into contact with it burn away. Amazing as it sounds, they let us onto the wards to clean the drains while people were recovering from operations.

In complete contrast to my day, soon after I got home that evening, Tony rang to ask if I wanted to go to a drinks party that EMI were hosting. It sounded like a lavish affair: he said there would be a lot of celebrities there, press photographers hanging around the door, bouncers to stop gatecrashers. Obviously, I jumped at the chance to go.

It certainly was magnificent. George Harrison and John Lennon arrived in the most outrageous suits, the champagne flowed like water and there was every kind of food and drink imaginable. Everyone seemed to be enjoying it, and then George Harrison came strolling over. 'Boring fucking party!' he said.

I must say I was a bit surprised since I was thinking it was great, but then I hadn't been to that many. Tony asked George about the Beatles latest recording, but George looked indifferent and just mumbled something.

'Do you ever miss just going down to the pub and having a drink?' I asked.

'Bloody right!' he exclaimed, finally animated.

'If you weren't dressed like that, we could go and have a beer somewhere,' I said, the words out of my mouth before I had time to think.

Tony looked shocked but George laughed and said, 'I'll go and get changed then!'

He came back twenty minutes later in an ordinary black suit and sunglasses and led Tony and me out of the building without a word to anyone. I did notice one of the waiters wearing George's suit!

'Are you 'queer'?' George whispered to me as Tony got in the first round at the pub.

'Fuck off!' I said angrily, glaring at him. 'No, I'm not!'

'Why the fuck are you hanging around with *him* then?' he asked.

'He's my friend,' I said, feeling sorry for Tony and not wanting to say anything that might hurt his feelings, but sweating a little with nerves. I was only sixteen, in awe of George Harrison. 'I know he's queer,' I added, 'but he knows I'm straight, so it doesn't matter to me and it shouldn't matter to you.'

'All right!' he said, putting his hands up.

It was a strange evening. Nobody took any notice whatsoever of George. We had a couple of pints in the first pub and moved on to the next one. George didn't have any money on him, which he was initially very embarrassed about, but he was a big star and it was understandable: the Queen never carries cash either! I was getting such a kick out of the fact that I was having a laugh and a joke with one of the Beatles that I could not have cared less about the money. George didn't seem relaxed around Tony though, and the more he drank the louder he became, frequently asking Tony what it was like being 'queer'. Tony had no answer, and I didn't come to his defence, which I should have done. He just stood there, looking increasingly uncomfortable, until, finally, I thought it was time to get George back to the party.

Tony was very quiet on the way home and I asked him what was wrong.

'I don't think we should see each other anymore, Steve,' he said.

I understood, then, that he was as upset with me as he was with George. By not speaking up for him, it was as if I was condoning George's attitude.

'Don't be stupid!' I replied, trying to make light of it. 'George didn't mean to hurt you.'

'He did,' he said, looking at me with complete dejection in his eyes.

I knew he felt I had let him down badly, although, I can honestly say with my hand on my heart, I do not believe George meant any harm.

The next day, I was full of it. I met Ron in a coffee bar in St Martins Lane and I could not wait to tell him what had happened the previous evening. After wittering on about it at length, I realised that Ron did not believe a word and was just humouring me by listening. We spent another day cleaning drains in the hospital with *Blue Devil*, which was enough to bring me back down to earth with a thud. At the end of it, Ron informed me that I would have to come back the next day and do the job on my own as he had been moved on to another one.

Feeling a little apprehensive, I arrived at the hospital maintenance department the following morning. The man Ron had introduced me to, but whose name I couldn't remember for the life of me, was sitting in his moth-eaten chair. He asked me where Ron was and when I told him he chuckled to himself and said there was another department with blocked drains. Getting out of his chair, he motioned for me to follow him. We walked down a narrow corridor where the smell of chloroform was so strong it made me feel queasy and light headed. It seemed to take forever to get to wherever we were going.

'There's a water tank along here that needs some attention. Would you be able to take a look?' he enquired, as we were walking along.

'Yes, I can do that for you,' I said, thinking the location was strange because water tanks are normally on roofs.

When we finally went through a door, the smell nearly knocked me out. I could hear a drill whining away, and I asked if someone else was already working in there. He said there was, but he was acting very cagey about telling me who it was or what they were doing. We walked into another room that had two wooden tables in the middle of it, and on the tables were two bodies. Someone was drilling open the head of one of them.

I don't remember much else, just a hand smacking my face and the maintenance man looming over me. 'Get up, son! You'll be okay!' he was laughing. He helped me to my feet and I was promptly sick all over the floor. Again, he laughed.

'Get him out of here, and clean up that mess!' shouted one of the people who had been doing the drilling.

The maintenance man took me to another room at the back where I could wash my face, and he told me to get straight back into the first room or I would never get up the nerve to go in there again and would be no use to any hospital. Still feeling very queasy, I went back.

'Well done! You've passed!' said one of the two men now clapping and laughing.

'Come over and we'll show you what we're doing,' beckoned the other.

I walked over to where they had been drilling the head open, and one of them explained that his job was to prepare bodies for post-mortem. He was a mortician and he had to remove the top of the skull so that the pathologist could remove the brain, weigh it and take samples, hopefully enabling him to find out the cause of death. For some reason, I was interested and felt better than I had half an hour before. I could actually look at the bodies and not feel sick. The mortician then told me something that has stuck with me ever since: 'When you see a dead body, remember it's just like a robot with a battery for a heart. When the battery runs down the robot is finished.'

I saw a lot of dead bodies during my time of working in the hospital, but one in particular affected me badly. I was working in a room next-door to the cold room where they kept the bodies, when a porter wheeled in a trolley and informed me that he had to leave it in this room for the mortician to collect. Being me, I could not help but look at what was on it. It was the body of a woman, aged about twenty five, encased in a plastic bag. Her stomach had been cut open and stitched up with such big stitches that I could see her intestines. That was bad enough, but alongside her, in another plastic bag, was the body of a perfect baby. Seeing the baby was too much for me: I couldn't help but cry. I still think about that woman and her baby, even now. Apparently, she had died during childbirth and they had been too late to save the baby. I remember thinking, how could there be a

God? Little did I know what I was going to see in years to come.

We worked on the outside of the hospital as well, and the guys would want to go for a pint. I wasn't a big drinker so I stayed on the job, which was at the top of the building. I wasn't strong enough to pull myself up there in the cradle though (we had to do it by hand; nothing was mechanised); they would pull me right to the top, tie the whole thing off at the bottom and then go off to the pub. I was working on a four inch cast iron drainpipe, using a paraffin blowlamp to burn out the lagging and old lead collars used to connect lengths of pipe in those days. I had to melt the lead and flick it out so that we could put in new lengths of pipe, or stacks, as they were called.

The guys came back after a few drinks one day, and thought they would have a laugh. I didn't hear them because of where I was positioned. They loosened the rope and slightly tipped the cradle with me in it. It gave me such a fright I let go of the blowlamp, which dropped, hit the pavement and exploded. They were annoyed because blowlamps were expensive, so they brought me all the way down at a sharp angle, with me screaming and hanging on for dear life. Then Ron, whose blowlamp it was, came and hit me!

He never missed a chance to have a laugh at my expense and the first job I did in Soho, famous for its strip clubs and prostitution, was a perfect opportunity. The job was in a very run down property with rotten timber frames and badly painted windows. There was a man standing outside talking to a group of men when I arrived. 'Come in,' he was saying. 'See what we've got to offer.'

The group just mumbled something and walked away.

'Fuck off then!' he said, under his breath.

I was very nervous, explained to him where I was from and told him that I needed to speak to Georgia. Instead of calling for Georgia, he shouted 'Mary!' through the door.

'All right, for fucks sake! I'm coming!' I heard a woman shout back.

Even coming from Kilburn, I had never heard a woman swear openly like that.

'What do you want?' she asked, appearing from behind the thick red curtains that were held by a brass pole just inside the door.

'I'm from Hutching and Kelsey, Miss. I'm the plumber.'

'Well, you'd better come in then.'

I followed her through the curtains into a dark reception area with just a few red lights on and loud music playing. We turned into a room where there were three girls stripping, a dozen men sitting in chairs watching them. I had never seen anything like it before and I was tempted to do a runner.

'Come on love, you can look at them later if you want?'

I must have gone as red as the curtains.

I only had to fix a small leak under the toilet, which I did as fast as I could and put my tools back in the bag; I wanted to be out of there as soon as possible. I stood up to look around for Mary and tell her I was finished.

'Hello, love! Are you looking for someone?' asked a scantily clad girl standing right in front of me when I turned around.

'I'm looking for Mary,' I stammered. 'I've fixed the leak.'

'Oh good! Mary sent me to find you. Come and sit down!' she invited.

'No, no, it's ok,' I said, embarrassed and petrified.

'How's Ron?' she asked.

'Fine.'

'We have an understanding with your boss: you provide us with your service and we provide you with ours,' she said suggestively, moving her hand towards my fly. 'Don't worry! Relax! I'll give you the same service as Ron has.'

Without another word, I ran, bouncing off the walls as I went. I managed to get to the front door, pulled back the curtains and bumped into Ron and Mary, who were laughing so hard they were doubled over.

'Did you get your payment?' Mary managed to say.

'No,' I said, clearly embarrassed.

They laughed even harder. Then I suddenly realised that in my haste to escape I had forgotten to pick up my tools. Ron made me go back and get them!

I had not attempted to contact Tony for a couple of months after the episode at the EMI party, and I felt guilty about it. I rang his house one evening, and left a message with his friend Julian, who told me he was sure that Tony would want to see me. He also said that Tony was in rather a state, but he would not go into any more detail than that. When Tony didn't ring back that evening I was worried about him, and, after finishing work the next day, I decided not to wait for his call, but just to go and see him. His car was not outside when I arrived but Julian opened the door.

'Hello Steve. Come in. Tony's not here but you can wait; he won't be long.'

He made me a drink, we sat down by the fire, and he immediately started telling me how moody and distant Tony had been since we had last gone out. Before he could say anything else, the front door slammed and Tony came in. When he saw me, he looked very pissed off.

'What the fuck do you want?' he questioned, standing looking down at me.

'I came round to see if you're okay,' I said, taken aback by his attitude.

'I don't need you or anyone else worrying about the likes of me,' he threw back at me.

'Come on, Tony! Steve has come to see you,' Julian said.

'I don't want to see him!' Tony retorted.

I stood up defensively and started to walk out. Tony turned around and grabbed my jacket. I thought he was going to hit me, so I instinctively ducked to protect my face.

'Do you think I'm going to hit you?!' he exclaimed.

I shrugged my shoulders, embarrassed, and then immediately astonished, when he then flung his arms around me and started to cry.

'Why did you not ring me?' he sobbed.

'You told me not to,' I reminded him. 'You said it would be better if we didn't see each other again.'

After a while he calmed down and took himself off to the toilet while Julian got me another drink. On returning, he seemed in a much better mood; in fact, he was quite cheerful and talking non-stop. 'I have to tell you: I'm in love with you, Steve!' he suddenly announced.

I floundered for a second, not knowing what to say, wanting to let him down lightly. 'You know I'm straight,' I said, as gently as I could. 'I've never let you believe anything else.'

He nodded quite affably, apparently relieved just to have got it off his chest, and carried on chattering. Every twenty minutes or so, he went to the toilet, each time coming back happier than before. I had no idea what was going on, until, during one of Tony's absences, Julian explained that he was going to the bathroom to do cocaine and had been using for a long time. I was very naïve: I had only ever read about drugs - never taken any. Julian also told me that Tony had tried to stop taking it but had become very depressed.

When I confronted Tony about it, he hit the roof, telling me to mind my own business. I knew then that he needed help, but I was not the one experienced enough to give it to him. I backed off and we both calmed down, ultimately agreeing that, given the strength of his feelings for me, it would be best if we stayed away from each other.

I never heard from him again.

Eventually, he was admitted to a rehabilitation centre and came out months later, seemingly free of his dependency. But then, when I was visiting Abbey Road some years afterwards, I was told that Tony had died as a result of drink and drugs. He was only twenty nine years old. To this day, I feel sad that I never even knew he was ill. He was a very special friend and I had a deep affection for him. He was a kind and gentle man who showed me how to be gentle and kind. I don't think it would have taken much to become infatuated with him and his lifestyle of money and excess, but I liked him too much to exploit his feelings for me.

Whatever God he had, may he watch over him.

The plumbing company was very good to me. I stayed with it and was trained to become a successful jobbing plumber, which I've had reason to be very thankful for more than once in my life.

The company used to look after most of the theatres in the area, and I remember seeing Sir John Gielgud rehearsing *King Lear* at the Coliseum in St Martins Lane. I sat in the shadows in my overalls, listening to the words of Shakespeare, thinking how beautiful Sir John's performance was. I was supposed to be unblocking the gents' toilets, and I was so engrossed in what was going on, on stage, that I didn't notice anything else.

'Are you enjoying it?'

I spun round guiltily and instantly recognized the comedian sitting behind me.

'Do you like Shakespeare?' asked Frankie Howard.

'Yes, I do!' I enthused, at the same time thrilled to be speaking to yet another celebrity. 'It's the first time I've ever seen or heard Shakespeare. I'm actually only here to unblock the gents' toilets,' I explained.

He found this highly amusing and laughed so loudly that one of the actors on stage shouted for us to be quiet. We had a bit of a chat and he seemed like a nice man, but when he asked me if I wanted to go for a drink after I had finished the toilets, I turned him down. I was a bit more worldly-wise by this time and realised he was gay. The attention was beginning to make me wonder if I might appear gay, not that it bothered me because I got a kick out of mingling in the show business world, even if it was just at the outer edges.

I later worked at the London Palladium for about three months, at the same time as Cliff Richard was in pantomime, and every lunch break I would run down to the wings and watch what was happening on stage. The director sent for me, one day, and I thought, *what have I done now?* As it turned out, one of the extras had not shown up and they needed someone to stand in; he did not have to ask me twice! I was so excited I could not wait to tell all the guys on site. The foreman said he would have to ring the office and get permission, which worried me a bit in case it wasn't given, but there was no problem and the boss even said he would come to the performance.

That afternoon, I saw my costume: I was going to be a cat! The only thing you could see of me was my eyes, and the only thing I had to do was walk around in the background, which anyone could manage. All I can remember of my performance is how hot it was in the costume. Still, how many plumbers have been in a cat costume on stage at the London Palladium?

The next day, the guys on site gave me a present: two tins of cat food!

# Not Ma

After working as a plu
I decided to go back
brothers' business had ............moved to
Kings Cross, purchased ...........ouse and another five
machines, and now employed seven men.

To work in printing, you had to belong to a trade union called the National Graphical Association, and it was through this that I also got my first job working for the national newspapers. My brothers did not work for the Press, but when newspapers were short staffed they called in other NGA members, like me, through the shop stewards. It was an occasional job that involved throwing newspapers, from a van, at all the major train stations. And it was a strange set-up.

The first time I arrived at a newspaper office (which shall remain anonymous) I was told to go and see the Father of the Chapel (FOC), a title that dates back to the time when printing was controlled by churches. In the NGA, the Father of the Chapel was the union representative – the shop steward – for a particular area or office (if it was a large one), and in this newspaper office the FOC was God! He took my name and asked to see my union card because in those days it was verboten to work in the newspapers

the NGA. After thoroughly
said 'You're John Wilton.' I was
dn't dare ask questions. The size of
alone was rather daunting for a young
little experience of life. I had never seen
g like it: massive metal staircases reached as
as the eye could see, and machinery, with men
perched beside all the moving parts, hummed
constantly. It reminded me of a big gothic castle with
images of past years carved in stone. I'll never forget
the smell of white spirit, printing ink and the heady
fumes of machine oil.

I followed Jack, the young guy who was
showing me round, through a labyrinth of corridors,
which seemed to go on forever. While he was
explaining that I would have to pay five pounds out
of my wages to the Father of the Chapel, I was
wondering if we would ever reach our destination.
The noise was deafening, and most of the men
working there had ear protectors on. When we finally
arrived, I could not believe what I saw: conveyor
belts going up, down, sideways - *all* directions -
carrying hundreds and hundreds of newspapers.
Every so often, a man would take off a certain
number and pass them on to the next man and so on,
in a chain. My job was to stack the papers into piles
and load the vans, which were waiting to deliver to
the stations.

At the end of the night shift, I went to pick up
my wages. Not really knowing what was going on, I
arrived at the FOC's office.

'How did you find your day?' he asked.

'Fine thanks,' I replied.

'What's your name?'

'Steve Grayson.'

'Your *name*!' he emphasised with a scowl.

'Oh yes, Sir! Sorry, I forgot. John Wilton.'

He handed me my wage packet and told me to open it. I couldn't believe it when I saw it contained twenty pounds for four hours work. My brothers only paid me thirty pounds for a whole week. The Father of the Chapel coughed while I revelled in the sight of the money.

'Well, come on! Pay up!' he demanded.

Five pounds was a lot of money to me but I handed it over without a word. 'Keep your mouth shut, and your eyes open,' my dad had said.

I later found out that there would be no record of me having worked there, but I'd get my money and the FOC would get his cut. Although the newspaper had called me in, nothing was ever checked. There was a lot of nepotism and fiddling in the union in those days, and big money involved, which is what ruined it in the end. In one newspaper office the FOC had a Mark 10 Jaguar and parked it in one of the directors' reserved spots. That caused questions! And things like that soon gave the game away.

That was my introduction to the newspaper business.

It was 1965 and I was about to add another experience to my eighteen years of life. I'd met Maureen a couple of years before at a dance at the Lyceum. The girls always stood on one side of the dance floor and the fellows on the other, then. We would eye each other up, and, if we saw someone we fancied, we had to walk across to ask her to dance, all the time hoping we would not get a knock back and have to crawl back humiliated. I was never backward in coming forward and I didn't have any trouble talking to girls; if I saw someone I liked I'd just go across. Jimmy Eat never could: he would turn to jelly, which doesn't really impress girls, so he'd ask me to go and 'pull' whomever he fancied for him, and I often did. I'm not being big headed or saying I was good looking. It wasn't about that. It was all about talking and joking and having a laugh.

When I met Maureen, I actually fancied her friend. I can't remember her name, but I was dancing with her when Maureen came up and said something to her. The music was too loud for me to hear what she said, but the girl nodded and went away, leaving Maureen to dance with me. It went from there: we struck up a relationship, got serious and saved up to get married. Jimmy kept on telling me I was too young to settle down, but of course I didn't listen to him.

Maureen lived in Welling, which was the country to me. Her father was a navigator in the war and a real RAF type. We got on very well, often getting drunk together. I was just a teenager, of course, and, one time, when we got back from the pub, I was so drunk that I felt sick and couldn't see straight. I stumbled up the stairs, bouncing off the walls, and managed to get into the bathroom, but my body had a mind of its own and I was banging against everything as if I was being pushed. I fell against a mirrored medicine cabinet and brought that crashing down, and then I threw up all over the place. I could hear Maureen having a go at her dad for having got me so drunk, so I was relieved that at least he was getting the blame! Maureen came upstairs to the disgusting state of the bathroom and me being *so* ill, but she did not get mad with me. That was love!

She did actually finish with me once. She didn't give a reason: she just said she didn't think we should see each other any more. We had been going out for months by then and I could not understand it; it really upset me. She worked at Africa House in London and I kept ringing her there, and then I went to see her... I just pestered her until we got back together!

The big day arrived. I looked and felt a million dollars in my new maroon mohair suit and lovely knitted tie. But Jimmy wasn't the only one who was none too happy to see me settle down. On the way to the registry office, my brother was driving ahead in his beautiful Metropolitan and I was sharing the car behind with my mum and dad. He suddenly stopped so we pulled in behind, wondering what was wrong. Sam leapt out and ran back to us as I wound down the window.

'Steve, you don't have do this,' he said, looking very serious. 'You've still got time to change your mind.'

Looking back, maybe I had an inkling that I was too young for it to work out because the conversation went on for about twenty minutes, and was more about how I could not do that to Maureen than about how much I loved her and wanted to marry her. I was twenty minutes late, but we did get married.

We had our reception at the furnished flat we had just rented in New Cross. It wasn't much: the furniture was extremely old and we shared a toilet and bathroom with the people downstairs, all for the princely sum of five pounds a week. The reception had not been long underway when my dad announced that he had a football match to go to that afternoon. My dad and brothers never missed a Queens Park Rangers match, even on my wedding day. The sausage rolls went and so did they!

On the whole the marriage was a happy one, but I was only eighteen and not really ready for responsibility. Maureen took care of the money: I handed my wages over every week and she gave me a couple of quid back for lunch and the tube to get to work. We hardly ever went out because we were saving for a house, and any spare money we had went into a building society, or Maureen would buy china and glassware, which we never used; it was put away under the bed or in the wardrobe for when we had our house. I also bought her things for this collection: brandy glasses or a fruit bowl in Waterford crystal, because it all had to be good stuff. With the money I earned working for my brothers and the newspapers, we were managing to put away quite a bit each week and we did look at houses, but none of them were clean enough for Maureen! There was always something she didn't like.

After four years, the cracks began to show. When I was working nights I began to drop into the local pub, the Rose Inn, to have a couple of drinks. They had a tombola and the guy who organised it asked me if I wanted to call the numbers. I told Maureen because I thought I would be earning a bit of money, but she was more concerned about me being in a pub; she didn't like it. I did it anyway, because of the money. But there *was* no money. Payment was in drinks! I had only had one that night, which I'd paid for earlier, and I couldn't have any more because Maureen would have gone potty. Maureen went potty anyway, because there was no money! In the meantime, the pub had agreed to keep the drinks for me, and I could go in and have them whenever I wanted. This became a regular thing for a while, because I thought of a way the pub could earn more money from the tombola. I could never tell Maureen, of course.

I happened to meet some people there, one night, who invited me to a party in the Jamaican area and I went. There were a few white people there, but not many, and I had a fabulous time. The mother had made a chicken stew with curry and spices, and everyone just dipped into it and ate standing up. I got chatting to a girl and I liked her. I wasn't trying to get off with her, but I began to wonder what I was missing. I realised I did not want to be in a little flat with a bit of music and nothing else happening; I wanted to be out enjoying myself. I did not want to hurt Maureen but there was a world out there and I hadn't seen any of it. I was bored, not with Maureen but with marriage and the organised, routine life of saving for a house that never came. It's not much of an excuse, but it's the only one I've got.

I started going out more, not to meet women but to enjoy myself, and I started drinking more heavily. One night, I went to a club called the Bird's Nest, in Waterloo. It was not a very big club but it had the right name: there were so many unattached women there, let's just say you didn't need a net to catch one! It was like breaking into a confectionary shop! Of course, I met somebody, and it was such a nice relationship I can't even remember her name! I only saw her a few times and I liked her, but anybody would have done. I didn't like myself for doing it, and I mean that sincerely. I was a coward: I couldn't tell Maureen what was going on and I was lying to her more and more.

Then I met Richard, who helped to speed the downfall of my marriage. He worked for a mini cab company I used when I was working late at the newspapers, so I knew how much the fare was from Fleet Street to New Cross. He tried to charge me extra and I refused. He started to bullshit me, saying there had been lots of traffic, but I dug my heels in and told him to get his boss on the radio. He became quite aggressive so I got out of the cab, saying I was going to ring his boss. At that point, he called me back and apologised, explaining that he was only trying to make a living and offering to buy me a drink. I could see myself in him, trying to make a few quid, so I waited until he parked the cab and we went into a pub. We got along well and we stayed there until closing time.

By this time, the pubs I drank in were mainly in Fleet Street, the heart of the newspaper business, and after a few Friday nights, drinking together, Richard and I decided to go to the Bird's Nest. From then on, things went from bad to worse until I was woken, one morning, by Maureen slapping me across the face. 'You bastard!' she shouted. She had woken up and seen a love bite on my neck. I tried, unsuccessfully, to convince her that I had been stung by a bee! Even as I was saying it, I knew how ridiculous it sounded. She opened the bedroom window, took off her wedding ring and threw it as far as she could. Although I didn't realise it at that moment, she was ending our marriage in the most graphic way possible for her. She refused to speak to me all day; she just made a lot of phone calls and then left. I rang her parents' house on Sunday to see if she was there and was okay, and spoke to her mother, who simply stated that Maureen did not want to speak to me.

Next, I drank my way from New Cross to Stonebridge Park and arrived at my parents' house at about 11pm. All the lights were out. I knocked on the door, loudly, and then I knocked again. Finally, the lights went on and my mum opened the door. 'Whatever is the matter, Stephen?' she asked, not knowing whether to be angry or anxious, since I'd obviously been drinking.

'Maureen has left me!' I wailed, slumping in the doorway.

'Come in, but be quiet! Your dad's in bed,' she said, taking my arm to steer me into the house. 'You'd better go to bed, too,' she added as she shut the door. 'We'll talk about it in the morning.'

I didn't want to talk about it. How could I tell my mum what I'd been doing?

'What the bloody hell is going on?' my dad called as I walked up the stairs to my old bedroom.

'Sorry, Dad. Maureen's left me,' I moaned, standing outside his door.

'Go to bed!' he said, a man of few words, as usual.

I left the house early the next morning and went straight to work, hoping that Maureen would be back by the time I finished and got home.

71

The last thing I expected was what I saw when I opened the door that evening: the place was empty except for the old furniture that had come with the flat and some empty cardboard boxes. She had taken everything. Not that I cared about that; I just wanted her back. I rang her parents' house and her mother told me Maureen would still not speak to me and was not coming back, so I asked to speak to her dad.

'What have you done?' he said. He was a man's man and spoke quietly into the phone, his tone neither judgemental nor angry - more like he was talking to a naughty boy than his daughter's adulterous husband.

'We-ll ...' I began.

'There's no point in trying to lie your way out of it,' he said. 'You know that don't you?'

'I know,' I said, feeling sorry for myself.

'Just let things quieten down a bit, and I'll see what I can do.'

He couldn't do anything. I made numerous phone calls to the house after that, but Maureen would never speak to me. She did not mess around: it was one strike and you're out. They were tough days for me: I lived like a tramp, eating any old rubbish and drinking heavily. Richard suggested moving in to help out with the rent, but I still hoped Maureen might come back.

After a couple of months, I managed to speak to her while she was at work, and she agreed to meet me for a drink. I could not believe my luck, and I was sure she would come back to me. (I can't believe how conceited I was back then!) I dressed to the nines, with plenty of Brut aftershave for good measure, and took her to a restaurant. She seemed pleased to see me and we chatted quite happily; in fact, I thought it was going so well that I asked her to come back. She was very non-committal, at first, but I persisted, asking her again and again until she gave me a definite yes.

'When?' I asked, absolutely elated.

'Soon,' she said. 'I'll ring you next week.'

When I walked her back to the station, her train was at the platform and we ran for it. 'Why don't you come back now?' I gasped as she was boarding the train.

She shut the door and pulled down the window. I went to kiss her, but she pulled away. 'I'm not coming back to you, Steve.'

'What!' It was as if she had hit me; I was stunned.

'I've changed my mind. I'm not coming back to you,' she stated flatly as the train started pulling away.

I watched the train leave the station and then looked down at the rails. I thought about jumping under a train. I felt like my insides had been pulled out and I wanted to die. Being a coward, I headed for the pub instead and sat in a corner, drowning in my own despair. Full of self-pity, I kept thinking *how will I live without her?* I could not quite take in that this had happened and I managed to convince myself she *would* come back to me, one day.

She never did. She started divorce proceedings.

I know it was my fault and she didn't deserve what she got. I do believe that women are often on a higher plane and more mature than men, who just want to play about at that age. But I like to think that if the tables had been turned, I would have given her one more chance. With hindsight, of course, I can see she did me a favour. We wanted different things out of life, and it never *was* going to work.

# 6

# From the Ridiculous to the Sublime

Maureen and I split the money that we had saved for a house. We needed a couple of thousand to pay for the divorce, but we were each left with enough to keep us going for quite some time. I should have been sensible and put down a deposit on a flat or a house, but who's sensible at twenty two? Richard had moved into my flat and we were still going out drinking and trying to pick up anything with a pulse. It was a freezing cold flat in winter, and we used to huddle around the two bar electric fire to keep warm. We also shared a bed for extra warmth, unless we had brought girls home.

Living together in the small one bedroom flat, we often got on each other's nerves, plus Richard was always broke and we began to argue about money, actually nearly coming to blows, once, over a tin of sardines that he had bought and I had eaten. He decided to go to Jersey to work in a bar or a hotel and I thought I would miss his company, but I didn't. I carried on as usual, working for my brothers and drinking heavily.

One evening, when I had been working late at the newspapers, I met a guy called Ian in the pub. I had seen him driving one of the vehicles at work and we had a few drinks together. He happened to mention where he lived, which I thought was strange because it was an expensive area. When I commented, he said he did a bit of selling, and then roused my curiosity even more by being very cagey about what he sold. It took a few more meetings in the same pub before he told me that it was drugs. I was astonished; he looked like an ordinary, hardworking guy, not what you would imagine a drug dealer to look like. Looks can certainly be deceiving, I thought - a fact I would come to frequently exploit in my life. It didn't really matter to me what Ian did though, because I wasn't going to get involved.

Some weeks later he invited me to a party at his place. Never one to miss a party and curious to see if his house lived up to the expensive Hampstead neighbourhood it was in, I went. It did! It was fabulous and definitely had not come from the money he made driving a van. Sitting in a beautiful big garden, it had four or five bedrooms and as I stood looking at it I thought, *Christ!* How can he afford this?

When I walked in, it was like walking into a time warp, the furniture was so heavy and old-fashioned. It was good stuff but it didn't look right or go with him, even though he was perfectly comfortable with it. I didn't feel like I was in his house; it was like walking into an old person's house that he had bought and left as it was.

I met his wife and several of his friends, one of whom was 'Sam Knight', a notorious villain from the East End, although the name didn't mean anything to me, then. Ian told me he and his mates were about to have a game of cards and asked if I wanted to join them.

'No thanks, I don't play,' I said.

'It's up to you,' he replied. 'It doesn't matter if you just want to watch.'

He led me into the dining room, where all his villainous mates were sitting around the table with bottles of whisky, but no cards. Ian shut the doors and drew the curtains.

'Come over here, Steve. Sit down,' said 'Sam Knight'.

It sounded like an order and I didn't like it, but there were six of them and only one of me, so I did as I was told.

'Ian has told me a lot about you,' he said. 'He says you're very trustworthy.'

You lying bastard, you don't even know me, I thought, looking at Ian.

If eyes could speak, his were saying 'please don't say anything'.

'Sam' went on to explain that a group in Belgium were processing cocaine into tablets thinly coated with paracetomol, so that they would look like over-the-counter pills and test as paracetomol if anyone got suspicious. He wanted everyone to put in a thousand pounds.

'I'll have to think about it,' I said, wondering, *what the bloody hell am I doing here? Why are they trusting me with this information?*

'Well, don't take too fucking long!' said 'Sam'.

Once the meeting was over, I cornered Ian in the kitchen. 'What the fuck have you got me involved in this for?' I asked.

He looked surprised and started going on about this big job I was supposed to have done a year before. To his stunned disbelief, I told him I had never done any illegal jobs and he must have me confused with someone else.

'What the fuck am I going to tell 'Sam'?' he spluttered, panicking. 'He'll fucking kill me!'

Instead of leaving him to his fate, like a complete idiot I told him not to worry, I would explain everything and he would be fine.

Why did I *say* that? I was wondering, seconds later. Now I had to go and face this villain, knowing too much and not having any idea how he would react. I steeled myself and took 'Sam' aside. 'There's been a bit of a mix-up,' I began.

'What would that be?' he asked through narrowed eyes.

I turned on the charm and explained as best I could, adding that I thought it was a brilliant plan but I had no experience of this kind of thing and no cash to put in.

'If you repeat *anything* you heard in that room *anywhere*,' he said menacingly, 'I'll chop off your balls. It's only because I like you that you're keeping them now!'

He didn't have to tell me twice. And I still have my balls!

I was getting on all right on my own, although sometimes I missed Maureen. We had been married for nearly five years, so it was difficult to adjust, at first. I visited Abbey Road Studios once a week and drank with whoever happened to be at the bar. On more than one occasion, it was the band known as

Meatloaf. The lead singer, who also called himself Meatloaf, was quite mad, and we enjoyed some heavy drinking sessions together.

It was at the studios that I was introduced to Kate, a support keyboard player who was called in from time to time. We got talking and hit it off. She had a flat on the Kings Road above a pub, very convenient for me, as, obviously, I was now a very heavy drinker.

To say Kate was a live wire is putting it mildly: she was wild. She did have a boyfriend who was a musician, but she was a party girl and flitted all over the place. She also took drugs socially, although she was not an addict, and it was she who really introduced me to the world of drugs, which was very much part of the music scene. She laughed at my first dabble with cocaine because it made my mouth and throat numb, and I looked like a bumbling idiot when I tried to drink: I poured the stuff all over myself. Nor could I stop talking, and I found that I didn't need to eat or sleep. It was quite enjoyable, although it also numbed my nether regions, which wasn't a desirable side effect when you were with a girl like Kate!

She was a lot of fun – too much, sometimes – I never knew what she was going to do or say next. I went on seeing her for quite some time and managed to get through a fair bit of money because I acquired a taste for Bourbon. We would go to the studios and have a drink; there were always people around whom Kate knew and there were loads of great parties to go to.

It couldn't last, and it ended after a night when Kate was standing in as the support keyboard player at a Joe Jackson concert at the Apollo, Hammersmith.

We arrived early for the sound check and since she wasn't sure whether she would be playing or not, and we knew we had some time, we decided to get some air and do the usual things: have some drinks and top them off with cocaine. One thing led to another, which led to one pub after another and the inevitable happened: we missed the show. Naturally, Kate was really upset. The following day, after her manager rang her, and, for some reason, blamed the whole thing on me, things became strained between us. I had enjoyed myself with her, but I had no regrets because it wasn't real. I was enough of a romantic, even then, to believe a real relationship with a woman could not be built on shagging anywhere, anytime and looking for the next party.

I started flying to Jersey to see Richard, especially when there was a party, and I continued to sow wild oats, making up for what I'd missed by marrying so young.

Just after one of my trips, a friend called and asked me if I wanted to go to the BAFTA awards in Piccadilly. Although it was a very grand affair, the food wasn't up to much; the drink, however, was free, and drink was the only food I knew.

Carrying on from when I was a child, I always carried a camera with me wherever I went, and this occasion was no different. I was messing around taking pictures, when someone tapped me on the shoulder.

'Dear boy, are you a photographer?' he said.

'Yes,' I replied. I wasn't a professional but I took pictures and that made me a photographer in my mind.

'Well, would you mind taking a picture of me with my friend?'

I didn't realize who he was for a second, but then I remembered I had seen him on stage at the Coliseum, rehearsing *King Lear*. It was Sir John Gielgud.

'That will be half a crown,' I said, as a joke.

'Whatever!' he said, without smiling. That joke had obviously fallen flat!

After taking a few pictures of him, I explained to him that I didn't have the right camera on me, as I was a guest, but that I'd be happy to take some pictures with a proper camera another time. He thanked me and gave me the address to send the pictures to. I didn't expect to hear anything more from him. A few weeks later, however, I received a letter, thanking me for the pictures and asking if I would like to ring him and arrange a suitable time for both of us, when he would be only too pleased to sit for me again.

Well, you don't pass up on an offer like that, do you?

Sir John Gielgud lived in a three hundred year old mansion in Wotton Underwood, Buckinghamshire. The grounds were beautiful: well kept hedges, and lawns that looked like green silk. I arrived half an hour early, as I did not want to be late, and a butler showed me into a marvellous library that smelled of flowers and had walls full of leather-bound books. Sir John was sitting in a leather armchair, his hand outstretched. 'Steve, welcome to my home,' he said.

We shook hands and I sat down to talk to one of the most famous and respected of British actors.

We had tea, which the butler had brought in on a tray, and then I started taking pictures. I was having the time of my life, thinking, *how many people would love this opportunity?*

'Would you like to see the garden?' he invited, when I'd finished.

Naturally, I said I would.

'I would hate to see these pictures in some disgusting magazine,' he said as we meandered around the gravel pathways.

'I can promise you, you won't,' I assured him. (And he never did.)

I charged him the two shillings and sixpence of the failed joke, which he agreed was very reasonable.

# 7

# She Loves Me Not, She Loves Me

Some months later, Richard was back in England, living at the flat with me and working for *Melody Maker*, selling advertising space, when we came up with the idea of trying mobile disc jockeying in the evenings. We both liked music. How hard could it be? The only drawback was that we had no equipment.

There was no way we could afford the proper stuff, but Richard had a record player, and I had a brainwave: I went and bought one the same, built a box to fit them both, painted it black and set it all up. From a distance, it looked just like any other set of decks that I had seen.

We did a few bookings together, but it didn't last long. We kept on arguing about money and decided to split up and do it separately. That meant I only had one record deck, but I bought another one and got a friend, who was an electrician, to set up a 'sound to light' system so that lights flashed while the music was playing - all the rage in those days. I was doing all right, earning money from three sources: my brothers, the late night jobs for the newspapers, and now disc jockeying. Of course, I spent it as soon as I made it.

Richard and I usually went drinking on a Friday evening and ended the night at the Rochester Steakhouse. Being fed up with this routine one week, I decided to look up an old friend, Lynn, whom I had known at school through Barbara. She was a bit of a good time girl and I was sure she could cheer me up!

Richard dropped me off at her house on his way to the pub. Having known Lynn's father from years before, I had a good chat with him, but Lynn was out; she was at a friend's flat round the corner, he thought. He mentioned that the name of the friend was Jeannette, who had also been a school friend of Barbara's, so I walked round to the address he gave me.

A thin young girl answered the door.

'Is Lynn here?' I asked.

'She doesn't live here.'

'I know, but her dad said she might be here. Is Jeannette here then?'

'No, but she won't be long. Do you want to come in and wait?' She looked bored but stepped back to let me in.

Looking around, I was surprised at how messy the flat was, considering girls lived there. I had been brought up to believe that girls were clean and tidy, and Maureen, being very house proud, had done nothing to make me think differently.

'Do you want a drink?' she asked as I sat down.

'Thanks. I'll have a scotch, please.'

'We don't have any.'

The evening was not starting out all that well. I went to the nearest off-licence and bought some whisky. On my return, Jeannette still wasn't back so the thin girl and I finally got round to introducing ourselves. Her name was Chris and while we sat drinking she told me that Jeannette had been married and divorced, but her ex- husband still came round to see her sometimes. I wasn't really interested. Chris and I were getting on well and I was just out looking for a bit of fun. In fact, being young and conceited, I thought to myself, I could give her one. After all, I was very smart: I bought my suits from Kings Road, Chelsea, my shoes from Sloane Street, and I had a real suede coat from Austin Reed!

A little while later, the front door opened and in came two girls, Jeannette being one of them.

'Who are you?' asked the other one, as Jeannette hurried past and disappeared into another room.

'Steve. I came round looking for Lynn. Her dad said she might be here.'

'I'm Val. Nice to meet you.'

Jeannette came back and sat down. 'You look like someone I used to go to school with,' she commented without much interest.

'Who's that then?' I asked.

She looked at me with a bored expression. 'Steve Grayson.'

'I *am* Steve Grayson!' I laughed.

'I know you are,' she said.

She looked good and although she was very abrupt I really liked her the most, not that it mattered; they all looked good and I was sure I would have one of them in bed by the end of the evening. While we all chatted, I kept hinting at staying the night by looking at my watch and wondering, aloud, what time the trains stopped running. 'Do the trains run late here?' I finally asked, not getting any response to the hints.

Jeannette gave me a look of contempt. 'Of course they do! This is London!' she said rudely.

Not much luck there then! I thought. Still, there were the other two. We were sharing what was left of my scotch and because there was no other alcohol in the flat I concluded that they must not have much money. That was how I measured people in those days.

'Why don't you stay here tonight?' offered Val.

*Finally!* I thought.

They put a sleeping bag on the floor of the front room for me and then went to bed. I lay there, looking at the ceiling and thinking that any minute one of them would come in; I hoped it would be Jeannette. I waited and waited and must have dozed off because I was woken by a noise: someone was walking down the hallway to the toilets. I waited for the footsteps coming back, thinking this would be it. But she walked straight past! *What a cow!* I thought. I fell asleep again and was woken in the morning by another noise in the hallway. This time, I got up and got dressed. When I emerged from the front room, I found Jeannette with a vacuum cleaner in her hand and rollers in her hair, clearly not fancying me at all. She looked a right bloody mess and if looks could kill I'd be dead right now. Don't ask me why, but I still fancied her and tried to make small talk. She was so uncommunicative I thought *balls to her,* and when Val came out and asked me if I wanted some breakfast I followed them both into the kitchen for some cereal.

'I really don't feel like going to work today,' Jeannette said to Val. 'I hate working on Saturdays.'

'I'll give you a lift,' I offered.

'Do you have a car?'

'Not at the moment.'

'Oh, I've had enough of you!' she said dismissively. 'I'll get a bus, *thanks!*' she added sarcastically as she left the kitchen to go and get ready.

I was still waiting for her when she was ready to leave and I followed her out. 'I get taxis everywhere,' I explained. 'Come on, I'll grab us a cab and drop you off at work.' I ran down the street to try and flag one down, only to find that there was not one solitary taxi anywhere in sight.

'I'm getting the bus!' shouted Jeannette, not having followed me.

'I don't do buses,' I said, running to catch up with her.

'Who asked you?' she retorted, looking at me as if I was something stuck to the bottom of her shoe. 'No-one asked you to come.'

I got on the bus with her, anyway, and tried to talk to her, which was incredibly difficult as she could not have cared less whether I was there or not. When we got off at Oxford Street, still having half an hour before she had to start work, she went to look round a shop, with me meandering round with her. She stopped to look at some coats, one of which she seemed to really like.

'Would you like it?' I asked. 'I'll buy it for you.'

'No thank you.'

I had had enough. I was sick of trying. 'I'm off!' I announced.

''Bye,' she said with the disinterest I was now used to.

'I'll see you around,' I said, thinking *what a miserable cow*! and took myself off to the Kings Road to have a couple of drinks and buy a new pair of shoes.

When I got home I found Richard watching the television. 'How did you get on?' he asked.

I thought about lying to make myself look better but decided there was no point. 'Waste of time!' I said and told him everything, in particular how standoffish Jeannette had been and how I really liked her. 'I'm going to throw a party next Saturday,' I decided on the spur of the moment, 'and invite them all. You never know, you may be able to get off with one of them.'

Richard just shrugged, but he was always up for a party.

The following Saturday morning, I bought some red light bulbs, which were very popular then. I hadn't got round to inviting Jeannette and her friends yet, and hoped I hadn't left it too late when I rang the flat. I need not have worried: Jeannette wasn't there but Val said they would all come, as they had nothing better to do.

'Ask them to bring food for Sunday lunch,' Richard called from the background.

'I heard that,' said Val. 'What do you want us to bring?'

'Anything will do,' I said happily.

'Since we have to carry shopping for you, we'll get a cab,' she replied. 'See you later!'

I hadn't cleaned the flat since Maureen left and, looking around, I suddenly realised it was absolutely filthy and littered with empty milk and beer bottles. We put them in the loft and did a quick tidy up, hoping the red lighting would hide the dust and grime.

When the doorbell rang that evening, Richard suggested that we not go down straight away and then we might not have to pay for the cab. He was like that. But it was pouring with rain and I couldn't leave them standing there.

'Pay the cab!' ordered Jeannette, walking past me as soon as I opened the door.

*Fuck it!* I thought.

'At least they paid for that lot,' whispered Richard, when several bags of shopping were deposited in the kitchen. Wrong again!

'You owe us five pounds for the meat and three pounds for the vegetables,' piped up Jeannette.

*Fuck it once again!* I thought.

They asked when everyone else would be arriving. I knew there were only two other guys coming but I was not about to tell them that. I made some lame excuse about having just had a couple of phone calls from friends who couldn't make it. They looked at each other dubiously, as if re-thinking the whole evening. 'What would you like to drink?' I asked quickly as Richard put on some music.

As the evening wore on, I finally got to dance with Jeannette. A slow, sad song called *Gay* was playing. Romantic, I thought, my hopes rising, until I felt dampness on my neck. Looking down, I saw she was crying. 'Whatever is the matter?' I asked.

'This song reminds me of my husband,' she sniffed.

*Bloody marvellous*! I thought. The evening was really not going to plan. I had organized this whole thing for her and here she was, crying about her husband. I changed the record. 'This one reminds me of my ex-wife. Now we can both have a cry!' I said jokingly.

All of us guys tried absolutely everything we could think of to get our evil way with the girls. Nothing worked. They ended up sleeping in our bedroom on their own. To say we were pissed off was an understatement. We were even reduced to listening through the wall, but all we could hear was a lot of garbled talk and laughter. Although they cooked lunch for us the next day, I was convinced Jeannette was not in the least interested in me.

Nevertheless, I rang her several times during the week after the party and asked her out. She just kept making excuses so I took it upon myself to go round to her flat one evening. All the girls were in, but whoever else welcomed me Jeannette certainly didn't: I was met with her usual indifference. Nevertheless, I suggested she come with me to get a take-away. She remained non-committal and uninterested, whereas Val was eager to go with me. Any port in a storm! I thought. I was such a male chauvinist pig and Val obviously liked me. My only excuse is that I was young and I did have my needs!

I asked Val if she wanted to go for a drink first. She did, and we had a lot more than one. Walking back, sampling the take-away, I dropped grease and sauce down my suede coat, earning more disgusted looks from Jeannette when we got in, and then a few more when she saw what was left of the take-away. After she had eaten it, she said she was still starving but I detected a little more friendliness. Grabbing the moment, I asked her if she would like to go out the following evening to a good Indian restaurant I knew. Much to my amazement and Val's annoyance, she accepted.

'Great place this, isn't it?' I said, as the waiter showed us to a table the next night. 'It's quite expensive,' I added, hoping to impress her.

'I know, I came here the other evening,' she said, obviously *not* impressed. I could not do anything right with this woman!

The meal went well, however, and Jeannette softened towards me. Even so, I nearly fainted when I invited her back to the flat and she said yes. She actually stayed the night, and, over lunch the next day, she explained that she liked me but had thought I liked Val, until Chris convinced her otherwise. I was over the moon: Jeannette *liked* me after all.

Her background is very different from mine. Her father was a butler and her parents had an impressive home in Regents Park. The first time I went there for dinner, it was the classic nightmare: I was faced with an array of cutlery I had no idea what to do with and thinking, *oh shit!*, until Jeannette started giving me signals about what to pick up. She couldn't save me from embarrassing myself when we went to Somerleyton, however. Jeannette's father, who had worked at Somerleyton Hall years before and become a friend of the family, took us to see Dowager Lady Somerleyton. She had invited us for cocktails at her residence, the dower house, and, when I was offered a martini, I thought they meant Cinzano. I asked for a red one! I could see Jeannette and her dad cringing. Then I removed a cordon and sat in a beautiful chair, which turned out to be a coronation chair – and not to be sat on!

A few months later, undeterred, I invited Jeannette to move in with me and, funnily enough, she accepted. I cleaned up the flat as best I could and we had a lovely first weekend together. Then Monday came and with it the electricity bill, stating that we were about to be cut off. Jeannette was not best pleased, and I did a mad dash to get the bill paid. My worlds were colliding, which happened more than once in the coming weeks, mainly because Richard was still living at the flat.

Typically, in the early hours of one morning, the doorbell went, and as I went down to answer it, I could hear what sounded like a crowd of drunken football hooligans. I opened the door to find Richard and about twenty five fellows on the doorstep. 'I brought a few friends round for a drink. You don't think Jeannette will mind, do you?' said Richard, as they all trooped past me up the stairs.

They were all gay guys who had been at the Vauxhall Tavern that night. Richard was not gay, but I had introduced him to the Vauxhall Tavern a couple of years before, and he had had such a good time that he still went regularly. What could I say? I went into the bedroom to see how Jeannette was reacting to the commotion. She was awake and not at all happy. I put a shirt and trousers on, anyway, and went out to join the party. I did, however, turn the music down and tell everyone that they had to fuck off by 3.00am.

Eventually, Jeannette got up and came to join me. I thought she would still be annoyed but after a couple of stiff brandies she relaxed and got into the swing of things. On the stroke of three o'clock, though, the music was switched off, the vacuum cleaner and the duster came out, and no one would have known there had been a party at all, apart from the smell of cigarette smoke.

Richard soon moved out. It was a one bedroom flat and he was sleeping on the sofa, which I didn't mind because he was a drinking mate, but Jeannette didn't like it, which is understandable.

By then, Jeannette had met my parents quite a few times, but I wanted her to get to know them better, and vice versa, so I suggested to my mother that we come and stay overnight.

'There's nowhere for her to sleep,' my mother said.

'She can sleep in my room.'

'What? With you?'

'Mum, we live together!'

'Oh, all right, if you're sure.'

When we got there, Mum made her really welcome and it was all very easy and informal. So much so that Mum went upstairs later in the evening and came down with one of her nighties. 'Here you are, love,' she said to Jeannette. 'Steve said you sometimes sleep in the nude.'

My mum was only concerned about Jeannette being cold, but Jeannette was mortified and when we went to bed all she could think about was not making a sound in case my parents got any ideas about what we might be doing. *Do not move one inch!* she kept telling me. When a sudden knock came on the door, she jumped with fright and dived under the blankets.

'Come in!' I called.

'Sorry, love,' said Mum, putting her head round the door, 'I forgot to put the 'po' under the bed.'

I could not stop laughing as she came over to the bed and pushed a potty underneath it, while Jeannette curled up with embarrassment and scrunched down further under the blankets.

There were many such ups and downs, but we managed to survive them all for a good few years before I almost cocked everything up ... but that's another story.

# 8

# Enter Laura, my Lovely

We used to go for a drink with Richard at a pub called the London and Brighton, in Peckham, and we stayed for a 'lock-in' (after hours drinks) one night. It was held upstairs in a function room, which had a bar and a small stage. I immediately saw it as a great place for a disco and made the suggestion that we open a club; we could use my boxed record decks and Richard and I could take turns disc jockeying. All too easily, the pub landlord said we could rent it, on condition that he supplied the alcohol. The Sweet Pea Club was born! We went the usual route of getting my brothers to print leaflets and posters, which we put all round London, and we charged ten shillings entrance fee. Jeannette took the money at the door and we had a barman, George, who doubled as a bouncer. The rest of the time, he worked as a lifeguard at the local baths. He would have his way with girls on the top diving board – but that's by the by.

I was still working for my brothers, Richard was still with *Melody Maker*, and we had only opened the club on a few weekends when we decided to make a splash and hire a group. Richard, who knew all the good ones that were up and coming but not yet expensive, suggested a group called Blue. We got a demo disc, liked what we heard, booked them, put posters all over the place advertising the event and sold tickets in advance.

We got a good response and we were really pleased until Blue's manager rang to say something had happened and they couldn't make it. Panic! We had just one week to find another group! The only one we could get at such short notice was Belinza Cottage. We had never heard of it but were assured it was very good and a demo disc would follow in the mail. In the meantime, I got Sam and Ray to quickly print banners to put over all the posters, announcing that Blue was being replaced by Belinza Cottage. The day of the event came and the demo disc had still not turned up, but there was nothing to be done about that. Time had run out.

Imagine the scene that Saturday evening in Peckham, a rough area at the best of times: the place was jam packed; the atmosphere was hot and smoky (everybody smoked then); Richard was playing the music, and everyone was drinking, dancing and getting slowly pissed (I use the word 'slowly' because Bacardi and coke was the favourite drink of the moment, and we'd watered down the Bacardi in a continuing effort to maximise profits!). Time went on and the crowd was getting restless. Where was Belinza Cottage? We didn't know. They were an hour late and we had no way of contacting them. Eventually, they rang us. They had come from Brighton and were in London, lost. We gave them directions and Richard apologetically relayed the information to the punters, who were not happy: the rumble of discontent just got louder, so he put on more records and drowned it out with the music. They were not a polite or patient bunch.

Eventually, the group arrived and I told them to set up on stage behind the closed curtains while I went out front and gave them a big intro. I was so relieved I really laid it on thick, clapping my hands to get everyone's attention, waiting for silence, building up anticipation. 'We're very fortunate to have this group with us tonight. They've travelled a long way to be here,' I announced. 'It's been well worth the wait and you won't be disappointed. We're very happy and proud to announce...' A pause as the curtains opened, and then I shouted at the top of my lungs 'BELINZA COTTAGE!' Elvis Presley could not have had a better intro.

As I backed off to the side, I went cold. I could not believe what I was seeing ... and hearing. Violins! A cello! Belinza Cottage was a chamber music ensemble! The crowd was as shocked as I was, waited a moment – probably to see if it was a joke! – and then the first missile hit the stage. 'Get 'em off!' they were yelling, amongst other more colourful comments and demands, as they hurled bottles and glasses. The group picked up their instruments and fled (we never saw or heard of them again) and I was left to deal with this mob. There was nothing I could say or do except keep on ducking. A small fight broke out; people were running here and there: it was general chaos. Jeannette and George were useless - both drunk and just giggling the whole time. Fortunately, Richard and I were sober and we calmed everything down to a low growl by giving everyone their money back.

To round off the nightmare, for some reason – probably because we had just lost a lot of money - Richard suddenly accused Jeannette, who is painfully honest, of fiddling the bar till and drinking all the profits. Needless to say, I was not standing for that, so he and I then started arguing.

The bloom had gone off The Sweet Pea Club! It did not last long after that because we had more success as mobile DJs, working separately.

After much trying, Jeannette got pregnant in 1972, and we moved to the flat in Maida Vale where I had first met her. It was quite a small basement flat in a large Victorian house where Noel Coward had once lived. It's probably quite beautiful now, but at the time it was very dark and damp, and a home to mice. Fortunately, our cat, Max, took care of the mice.

Jeannette often came with me when I had a DJ booking, and, one Saturday, when she was heavily pregnant, I was booked to do a wedding in the East End. I had set up the equipment and we were sitting waiting for the wedding party and the guests to arrive. The bride's father had paid me up front, which was fortunate, given that I did not manage to do the job - through no fault of my own, I might add.

As people were coming in, Jeannette noticed the bride's father arguing with someone over a cigar: he was being persistent about offering it and the other fellow was refusing. The next minute the bride's father hit the other fellow over the head with a bottle. He fell to the floor as someone else leapt up and smashed a glass in the bride's father's face, after which all hell broke loose. Kids were screaming, there was blood and glass everywhere, and Jeannette ran forward to get the children out of the way. In her condition, it was no place for her to be and I told her to get behind our equipment. The mothers then started passing the children over to her so that she could put them out of the way before they – the mothers - dived into the fight! The bride also got involved and she soon had blood all over her wedding dress. It was an incredible sight! All over a cigar!

When the police arrived with ambulances, we were escorted out, and eventually it was all sorted out, but that was the last time I took Jeannette.

When she went into labour a few weeks later, it all went on for far too long and she had to have an emergency caesarean section. She insisted she wanted a 'bikini cut' and I told the surgeon this when they came to take her to the operating theatre. He said they didn't do it that way. I told him he was not having her unless he did, by which time we were running down the corridor. I kept on insisting and he kept on refusing. As Jeannette was taken into the operating room, I told him one last time not to cut her stomach upwards but to cut it at the bikini line. He actually did follow our wishes but I did not know that, and memories of the dead girl at the hospital, with the baby in the bag, came back to haunt me. I was worried sick until a nurse came and told me that they were both fine, and I had a little girl.

I went straight to the recovery room, where Jeannette and our little bundle of ginger fluff, Laura, were both fast asleep, oblivious to what was going on around them. Laura was the most beautiful thing I had ever seen in my whole life, and I suddenly panicked at the thought that this tiny life was mine. I was now responsible for these two women in my life, God help them!

When the surgeon, who was Greek, did rounds the next day, he said 'you were successful' to Jeannette, referring to the bikini cut. Because of his accent, she thought he said she was sexy. Of course, when she told me, I was annoyed and questioned him about it. And found out what he really said! One way or another, we left an impression.

I wanted to give Jeannette something more than the usual flowers, so I bought her oysters ... with a difference. She was in hospital for ten days and each day I sent her an oyster containing a real pearl. The time dragged for me, though, and I got fed up because it was a long way backwards and forwards to the hospital, and I wanted them home. When the day finally came, I was supposed to sterilise the bottles, ready for when they arrived - we had all these little sterilising contraptions that people had bought for us – but, in my excitement, I forgot. Naturally, Jeannette was furious, and also worried because she had never looked after a baby before. We ended up sterilising the bottles the old way, with boiling water. I was not a lot of help. I think I changed a nappy once.

Jeannette was a good mother but staying at home was not for her. Laura was not very old when we took her to a private nursery in St John's Wood, and Jeannette went back to work. Laura loved it there, so it was good for both of them.

I love giving presents, seeing the look on the person's face, and, because I didn't see a lot of Laura as she was growing up, I used to take her to the West End and buy her hand made toys from Galt's; she loved the bright colours. From Harrod's, I once bought her a monkey as big as herself. Recently, she said, 'Dad, when you die you won't leave me anything, and I don't want any of your crap anyway. But you'll leave me lovely memories and those are all I want.' That means so much to me because, although she wanted for nothing when she was growing up, I look back and see myself drinking like a fish and hardly ever home. She chooses to keep what's good, and has let me know that I have given her something worthwhile.

I bought countless presents for them at Christmas, and Laura always helped me wrap the ones I gave to Jeannette. They would be everywhere, and we had a lot of laughs, over-wrapping things and seeing Jeannette's frustration as she ended up surrounded in a sea of presents and paper. I often bought her clothes and handbags, which she 'loved' and then discreetly took back and changed! On one particular occasion, when I took Laura to Harrod's, there was a children's fashion show, which I let her stay to watch and then she picked out some stuff she wanted – none of which had a price tag. There was also a women's lingerie show, so I picked out a silk nightie for Jeannette. When we went to collect and pay for the clothes we'd ordered, I found that they cost a fortune. I paid for Laura's, but refused to pay the fifteen hundred pounds that the nightie cost. Laura started crying and said she wouldn't have hers then. That wasn't what was supposed to happen, so, after much negotiation, I managed to get the nightie for about six hundred. When I got it home to Jeannette, however, she didn't like it much and it didn't even fit her!

Jeannette is brilliant, considering all I've done to her, both good and bad. I've had a lot of money, lost it, made bad investments, given it away. It doesn't faze me because I know I'll get it again; it might take me a while, but I'll do it. But there are not too many women like Jeannette, whose attitude to material things is that they are just objects and nice to have, but she can be just as happy without them, and, if we need the money, sell them. She would also live anywhere: if I said we had to move to a one bedroom flat, she wouldn't like it but she would go. She's marvellous.

# 9
# An Unexpected Development

As if I did not have enough challenge and excitement in my life, in 1973 I decided to leave the safety blanket of my brothers' firm and go out into the world on my own. After Laura was born, we wanted to move out of the basement flat and thought about going somewhere outside London. I saw an advert in the Daily Mail for a printing job with Penguin Books in Thetford, Norfolk, and applied for it. They were looking for a machine minder, which doesn't sound like much but was a very specialised job (and, of course, this was pre-digital): the machine minder was responsible for setting up the print run on the machine and seeing it right through to the quality of text or pictures on the page at the end.

Penguin offered me the job, which meant moving to Thetford. The money wasn't very good but they would help with getting a house so we went to look around the area. It was suburbia: an overspill from London with new houses, modern pubs, and it wasn't for us. I was very chuffed to have been offered a job by Penguin Books, but I would rather have poked myself in the eye with a hot poker than live the nine to five suburban life, with my house tied into my job as well. I couldn't do it.

I got a job working for Austin Reed instead, printing their in-house leaflets. They were situated in

Carnaby Street, which I enjoyed because I love clothes and it was then the fashion centre of London.

By this time, we had moved into a large flat in a very prestigious Victorian mansion block in Castellain Road, close to where we were already living. We rented to begin with, but then got the opportunity to buy it for twenty five thousand pounds, which we were not sure we could afford. However, we decided to go for it and I think it was one of the happiest times of my life.

The responsibility of a family and a mortgage, and having to find ways to earn more money, was what first turned my interest in photography into something more commercial: I answered an advert in the local newsagents and got a job developing films for commercial photographers. It was all done through the post and I never actually saw anyone. I got films of the seaside resorts around England, developed them, printed them onto photographic postcards and sent them back.

Nobody had ever actually taught me how to do processing. Out of interest, I had picked bits up from reading magazines and listening to people. I also took the opportunity of learning whatever I could when I worked on the newspapers at night. It was all union controlled so I was not allowed to do anything, but I went into the dark rooms, watched and asked questions, and no one was too bothered. In particular, I saw how the film had to be put into a metal cartridge in a certain way, and I went away and trained myself to do that in the dark with an old roll of film. Then I had made a dark room at home and saved up to get the chemicals. They came with instructions, which were not very clear unless you knew what you were doing, so it was all trial and error and I often mucked it up, then got fed up because I couldn't afford to keep buying more film. Eventually, though, I got the hang of it and found it quite easy. Gradually, I learned how to improve negatives that were too dark or too light, and how to do enlargements. It was fiddly, but when something fascinates you that much you keep at it. When I saw the job advertised in the newsagents, I knew I could do it.

After a time, developing thirty or forty rolls of film a night became very boring. I carried on, because I needed the money, while keeping my ear to the ground and my eyes open for other opportunities.

Richard started seeing a girl called Karen, who worked for York records just round the corner from Austin Reed. Every so often, they had record promotions: big receptions for the stars, with, more importantly, free food and drink, and I was always invited. As luck would have it, I happened to meet Roy, the organizer who hired the disc jockeys, and he was talking about how much money could be made disc jockeying. I promptly told him I was a disc jockey and asked him to consider me if he needed anyone. He very courteously took my telephone number, and I thought that would be the end of it. I could not believe it when he actually rang one evening, told me he was seeing three new disc jockeys and asked if I would like to go. I jumped at the chance.

It was a very big nightclub, La Valbonne near Oxford Circus, and I had never seen record decks with so many knobs and sliders. Roy told me to have a little fiddle, get acquainted with it all, and he would be back in half an hour. I switched everything on and put a record on the deck. It didn't work, and I was still fiddling around, with not a clue what I was doing, when someone asked me if I needed a hand. I was about to say no, but thought better of it and admitted I had never worked that type of deck before. He showed me around the different controls, after which I shook his hand and thanked him; I was really grateful.

By the time Roy came back, I was ready to do a demo. There were three record decks and the trick was to keep the music running smoothly. Apart from a few minor mishaps, I thought I had done quite well. Even so, I nearly wet my pants when he asked me if I wanted to do the night shift. Bloody right I did! They were going to pay me fifty pounds a night!

Two days later, I walked into the darkened club, petrified, only having an hour to get ready for my shift and having been told that I would be controlling not only the music but also the lighting system, which I knew nothing about. I mentioned this to the DJ just finishing the afternoon shift. He was doubtful that he could show me everything in an hour, but, thankfully, he was willing to try. It was so complicated that I could not keep all the information in my head and had to ask him the same questions over and over. 'Right mate, you're on your own now. I'm finished!' he suddenly said, and left. I had a little fiddle around with the knobs and switches, fading up and fading down, but I soon ran out of time to try things out.

Because I was new, they had set up the records for me: there were three neat stacks of 45s and one of LPs. The moment came. I switched on the decks, faded up, and on came Gary Glitter. I remembered what I had learned two days before: once the record had started, the lights needed to go down. Looking at the control panel was like looking at that of a jumbo jet. Completely confused, I faded one up and one down. The music stopped! I panicked and started to sweat in the silence; all eyes were on me. I reached for the other slider and quickly pushed it up. There was a rumbling sound and the room started to fill up with clouds of dry ice, which gave me an idea. I stopped panicking, faded up the microphone and, in a fit of genius, announced to the audience, 'This is for Edward and Alexandra, who are getting married next week. May I be the first to congratulate them!' To my joy and amazement everyone on the dance floor started to clap and cheer and look around. There was, of course, no Edward and Alexandra but the place was too crammed with people for it to matter. I faded down the dry ice and faded up the sound, and the last few seconds of Gary Glitter blasted out.

It was an eventful night in more ways than one. Standing at the bar on my break, I struck up a conversation with a guy about twenty years older than me who seemed a misfit: he had a stack of books with him, tied together with a leather strap, which was not the sort of thing you saw in a nightclub.

'What time are you finishing?' he asked, when my break was over.

*Not that old line again,* I thought and quickly retorted, 'Look, I'm not gay!'

'No, neither am I,' he said, with a wry look. 'I just thought you did really well up there, covering up your mistake. My name is John North and I work for an intelligence agency. We're always on the look out for people who can hold their own in a tricky situation. I'd like to talk to you.'

A couple of days later, I met up with him in a steakhouse in Carnaby Street and he explained that his company did electronic surveillance. Not knowing what he was talking about, I asked him a lot of questions, most of which he answered, although the main one in those days was not what do you want me to do but how much will you pay me? As we parted company, he told me that it was best not to mention our discussion to anyone.

I did not see or hear from him for so long after that meeting that I assumed he had been talking a load of bullshit and was probably gay after all. I was wrong on both counts. John North would be back.

I carried on working at the club, going from strength to strength and thinking I was doing really well. It came as a shock, when, after four months, the manager called me into his office.

'Sorry Steve,' he said. 'We're going to have to let you go. Nothing to do with your work; it's just last in first out, I'm afraid. We'll give you a good reference.'

Needless to say, I was really upset. On top of my disappointment at losing a job I enjoyed, I was losing the money I earned from it. I no longer had the job developing films in the evening, so there was no option but to go back to being a mobile DJ.

My first job was yet another wedding reception. I told the fellow who called that the evening would cost sixty pounds with an initial deposit of thirty pounds, which I would come and collect. When I got there, I thought I had mixed up addresses because I was at the church where he had told me he was getting married. I knocked at the rectory door anyway, and explained why I was there to the vicar who opened it.

'It's me you're looking for,' he smiled. 'I rang you. This is my church and I'm getting married here.'

I should have taken that as a sign that more confusion might be on the cards.

The wedding was on a lovely, sunny Saturday afternoon. I had asked Stan, a friend I worked with, to help me with the equipment, and we arrived just after the ceremony when all the guests were having drinks. I set up the equipment on the stage and the vicar explained that he would like us to stay behind the curtains until he gave us the signal to open them. He showed me a button I would just have to press for them to open automatically.

When the signal came, I duly pressed the button. Nothing happened, so I shouted to Stan to pull the curtains. As he began to do that, the mechanism started to work and the curtains began to open. Because he had been drinking, either Stan didn't notice or was slow to react, or both, and did not let go straight away; he was still holding on to each curtain as they gathered momentum. Then it all happened: with arms spread wide, he fell head first off the stage and onto the food-laden head table set up directly in front of the stage. It was like the typical scene in a farce, but it was actually happening. In horror, I watched as the table - just a trestle – crashed, and everything went flying, including the wedding cake. Pandemonium broke out and the groom was raging.

I could only apologise, as Stan ran off to the toilets covered in egg salad. 'You don't need to pay me,' I said to the groom, to console him.

'Pay you?!' he spluttered. 'You should be paying me!'

Stan did not reappear and I had to quickly pack up the equipment on my own and leave, humiliated.

We met up in the car park and headed for the nearest pub. Many drinks later, I drove home. I was drunk, but Stan was worse, and I needed Jeannette's help to get him home. She was understandably angry. Apart from being woken up in the dead of night to take a drunk home, there was Laura to think of. I cannot remember why on earth we did not just leave Stan to sleep it off. However, I convinced Jeannette to help me. She got up, wrapped Laura in blankets and off we went. I only had a Mini Coop at the time and we had had to take the seats out to get the equipment in. Seat belts were still in the future, so there was Jeannette, sitting on the equipment clutching this tiny baby while Stan rolled around. She was absolutely furious and, quite rightly, vowed never to do it again.

A few days later, I did not think anything of it when I got a call from the Zambezi, a drinking club for South Africans and Australians in Earl's Court. They were looking for a disc jockey and I took the job, but it was not what I was used to: it was sleazy, dark and dingy; the record console was very old-fashioned and situated in a cubicle surrounded by reinforced glass - a goldfish bowl. When I asked about it, I was cryptically told I would be glad of it.

The first evening was an education. I sorted the records into chart order and started to play. Everything was all right to begin with and then, all of a sudden, there was a loud crash. Somebody had thrown a can of beer at the glass! Then another and another hit the glass. It went on and on. I switched on the microphone. 'What the fuck are you doing?' I shouted.

'We do this to every one. No one ever lasts out the week!' shouted back a girl in front of the screen.

Every time I put on a record, they threw a few more cans. I just ignored them. Then someone asked for the number one hit, which I had just played a couple of times on request.

'I'll play it again later,' I replied. 'People are going to get fed up with it.'

'Play something higher, then!'

'Higher than number one?'

'Yeah!'

They were all off their heads!

A few days later, I was getting myself together to go to the club, thinking, *here we go again!* when the telephone rang.

'Hello Steve, how are you?'

'Who is it?' I asked irritably.

'John North.'

'Oh yeah,' I said, my mood not lightening after the few seconds it took me to remember who he was. 'What sort of bullshit are you going to give me this time?'

'I don't bullshit, Steve.'

'Well, what do you want then?' I was running out of patience. 'I have to go and stand in a goldfish bowl and take a load of abuse. And I'm already running late.'

'Remember what I said about the surveillance work I do? Well, I've got some work if you're interested?'

Always interested in a job, I calmed down and arranged to meet him for coffee later.

Work at the club was a complete pain in the arse, as usual. I was relieved when I finally finished and went to meet John at a late night café. As we chatted, I realised he knew, without me telling him, that I had been asked to leave the first discotheque, and, on his own admission, he had not been in there looking for me, so they hadn't told him. A growing suspicion that he had somehow been responsible for removing me from there really pissed me off. I had really enjoyed that job, and was now having to suffer a living nightmare.

Meantime, he was explaining that he was employed by an independent agency that sometimes worked for some governmental department. He went into fine detail about the equipment they used, but still did not tell me the job he wanted me to do. I was generally confused, but especially so about why he was interested in me, and I asked him about it. He repeated that he and his colleagues had been watching me for a while and had seen the way that I was able to talk myself out of situations. I did not know whether to be pleased by the interest in me or angered by the interference in my life. Plus, I still thought this guy might be some sort of nutter. Every time I saw him, he was carrying a pile of books in a leather strap. They were never the same books and I had too many pressing questions to think of asking him about them. He must have been very well read.

On leaving, he gave me a telephone number, told me to think about what he had said and ring if I was interested.

Being of a curious nature, I rang.

# 10
# Undercover

His office was situated on the Charing Cross road, above a bookshop. It was difficult to get at as the council were digging up the road, repairing a leaking main, and a fire engine was trying to get through, causing absolute chaos. When I finally reached the door and rang the bell, John North's secretary answered in a clipped tone. I announced myself, and she told me to push the door and make my way up the stairs. I had expected a plush office suite. Instead, I was confronted with a dismal hallway, papered with woodchip and painted lime green. His office was not much better.

We talked for a while about the surveillance equipment before he introduced me to the technician who was to train me in the use of it. I was adamant that I would not give up my job at the club, awful as it was, because I needed it. He assured me that this was not going to be a problem.

Without telling anyone what I was up to, I trained for a month. The equipment consisted of electronic bugs, phone tapping equipment and video surveillance, none of which was as sophisticated as the modern equivalent, of course. The cameras were very large and they had to be hardwired back to the recorder; they were difficult to conceal and had to be put into televisions, radios or some other piece of furniture.

I carried on going to the club most evenings and it wasn't long before I found out why keeping that job had not been a problem: frequenting the club was a major drug dealer, the man under surveillance. He was probably the reason why I lost the job at the first club and had been engineered into this one, although it was never admitted.

Halfway through one evening, the target turned up, fat, bald and wearing a flowered shirt. Quite a number of the South Africans knew him, and I heard them calling him Barry White; the 'White', I later found out, being a reference to cocaine. I watched him handing the stuff over to his mates, who spoke Dutch. I had to tape the conversations, which was not easy, especially with the loud music, but I got enough for John to translate. Although most of the conversations turned out to be rubbish, we managed to get an address where he mentioned he was staying.

I went there early one evening with the technician who had trained me, our first job being to place a concealed camera and microphones. It was a flat above a shop on Willesden High Road. Filthy windows and grimy net curtains were set off by the typical rotten frames and peeling paintwork of a rundown property. We could not find a front or back way into the flat and surmised the entrance must be through the shop itself, which meant we had to get in under pretext. The technician said we would have to pose as some sort of engineers, and, in the back of his van, he had a suitcase full of different costume uniforms for rail, gas, water, telephone engineers, to name but a few. He decided on 'telephone engineer' and instructed me go in and pave the way, telling me it would be good experience.

Behind the counter in the shop sat a little Pakistani man. Decked out in the uniform, I told him that there was a problem with the main phone lines in the area, and we would have to shut down his phone for a few hours. He was annoyed, mumbling that he needed the telephone for his business. I apologised and asked if he owned the flat above, as we would have to check all the phones in the building to make sure they were properly off. He shook his head and said that the guy who rented the flat was out. I asked him, sympathetically, if he had a key because if he didn't and we could not get in that day, the lines could be down for a few days. Without further ado, he hurried away to get one.

The technician brought in all the equipment and it gave me a rush to be putting my training to use in a real life situation. A couple of minutes and we were out of there, but I was so nervous I think I lost a few pounds in sweat.

We sat in the van to await Barry's arrival. Around 11pm he turned up looking pretty drunk, swaying from side to side and tripping over now and then, and he had a woman with him. When they entered his flat, I couldn't believe the quality of the sound that was coming through the bugs. From what was said, we understood the woman was a prostitute who was giving him sex for drugs, and, at first, the technician thought we were wasting our time, as they'd probably have a shag and he'd fall asleep. But then they did a couple of lines of cocaine, after which Barry could not stop talking. He was recounting how big his well-connected family was back in Nigeria, and how stupid the British were because he was claiming social security he did not need. For most of the time, the woman stayed silent.

He continued talking about himself as if he were the most important man in the world, and then, out of the blue, he asked the woman if she would like to live with him. She faltered, as if she were thinking about it.

'Make up your fucking mind!' he yelled, taking offence. 'This could be the best thing you ever do in your life. I'm going to Portugal, and when I get back we could find a nice place to live.'

'Why are you going to Portugal?' she asked, possibly playing for time.

'If I tell you more about what I do, you'll see how much money I can make. But if you talk to anybody about it, it'll be the last thing you ever do!'

With that he gave her a blow-by-blow account of the drug operation, as if this would convince her to stay. 'We bring the stuff in every two months,' he said. 'It's so easy! The boss had a fibreglass boat built, and when it was being moulded he had secret panels built into the side below the water line. The only way they can be detected is if the boat is lifted out of the water, and even then, the panels would be almost impossible to see unless you knew they were there. We've already had the boat checked over by the police, and the silly bastards have given us a clean bill of health.'

'No they didn't!' I said aloud to myself.

'Yeah!' the technician joined in, as if we were in the room with Barry. 'We've got you on a long leash and you're going to lead us to the main man, my friend!'

Then everything went silent. The technician fiddled with some switches and looked around anxiously. 'Fuck! The power's gone down!' he exclaimed. 'We need to find out when he's going to Portugal. We'll never get this opportunity again. We'll have to put a sticky on the window tonight.'

(A 'sticky' is a small suction pad with a microphone in the middle that is stuck to a window in the room where the target is. When the target talks, the windowpane vibrates just enough to pick up the sound. In those days, everything had to be hardwired, which meant we also had to hide a wire somewhere.)

We waited an hour for the lights to go out; we waited another half hour, in the hope that they would be asleep. By now it was well past 1am and there was nobody about, apart from a few drunks. We had to be careful, however, because there was a police station at the end of the road, and we did not want them causing a scene and mucking this up.

We removed the ladder from the van and extended it up to the window, being careful not to make any loud noises. The technician held the ladder while I climbed up, sweating slightly with nerves, and peeped in; they were both asleep on sofas. I stuck the device to the window and gingerly climbed down. Then we hid the wire as best we could, connected the recorder to it and hid that in a dustbin near the main door. To prevent anyone spotting it, we could only leave it there while it was dark, so we only had until the sun came up to find out the date of the Portugal trip. To complicate matters, we couldn't listen in on this recorder and just had to hope that Barry would wake up and do some more talking.

It was frustrating, sitting in the van, waiting and hoping for something that might not happen. We decided we had to wake them up, somehow, without rousing Barry's suspicions, and we came up with the idea of getting a pizza delivered to the flat.

Twenty minutes later, a pizza delivery boy was ringing the doorbell. The lights went on in the flat, but, instead of coming down, Barry came to the window. He was inches away from the sticky. We held our breath as he opened the window. Thankfully, perhaps because he was half asleep, he didn't spot it.

'What the fuck do you want?' he shouted.

'I've got your pizza, Sir,' announced the delivery boy.

'I didn't order a pizza!'

'This is definitely the address I've been given.'

The woman came to the window and drew Barry back into the room before reappearing herself. 'It's all right, love, I'll be down in a minute!' she called.

After she had taken the pizza and gone back up to the flat, we re-checked the recorder, to make sure it was working, and then took turns sleeping in the van for what was left of the night.

The technician woke me when Barry came out of the shop and disappeared down the street. The woman was still inside the flat but we could not wait for her to leave: we had to remove everything before it was light and the shop opened. We retrieved the recorder from the dustbin and then had to tug on the wire to get the sticky off the window, risking the woman hearing or noticing the small movement. She made no appearance, so we assumed luck was on our side and she must still be asleep.

We went back to the van and listened to the recording, which was not very good but we could make out what they were saying. They had eaten the pizza, had a shag and taken more cocaine. As if on cue, Barry had once more started talking about himself and about the woman coming to live with him.

'Can I think about it and let you know next week?' she had asked.

'Yes, but not on Friday. I'm going to Portugal.'

Bingo!

Two weeks later, Barry and a Maltese man were arrested as they docked at Dover. The Maltese man turned out to be the boss.

# 11
# Graysons Home Services

By 1976 I had been promoted to print supervisor at Austin Reed. As should be clear by now, I was always trying to make extra cash, and I did some private printing, until the overall supervisor caught me printing cards for a carpet cleaning business. He told the personnel director and I was sacked.

I thought that was an end to it, but a couple of weeks later I opened the door to two plain-clothes police officers. They were very nice to me. I don't think it was the biggest crime they had ever had to deal with! Despite that, I was taken to the police station, questioned and put into a cell - locked up for printing business cards! I was released a couple of hours later and given a date to appear in court. I ended up with one year suspended sentence and an eight hundred pound fine, which was getting off lightly, according to the magistrate. He actually said to me, 'You should really go to prison, but we are going to be lenient with you.' Ha! I would have got less if I had stolen a car and run someone over! I found out afterwards that he was a personal friend of the personnel director at Austin Reed. Enough said!

After the court incident, with no real work to speak of, I decided to start up my own building and decorating business. It was a matter of survival. I called the business *Graysons Home Services* and offered every service I could think of: plumbing, building, painting and decorating, general maintenance, window washing and carpet cleaning. My brothers printed four or five different leaflets, all funny, and I put hundreds of them all round the posh areas. I soon got a call from the Advertising Standards Agency, telling me they had had complaints. On one of my leaflets was a picture of a bandaged tap with water running from it and the caption 'when you get old, you can't hold your water'. It was meant to be light hearted but had apparently upset a few elderly people. Naturally, I agreed not to put any more of them around.

I started getting work. I did anything anyone asked me to do and got people in to help me if I needed them. I got better at everything as I went along and made enough money to get a pre-cursor to the modern mobile phone: a big, heavy box with the handset on the outside and a giant aerial. It was expensive, but the investment was worth it because now people could contact me anywhere, anytime.

I was really pleased the first time I was recommended to a doctor in Harley Street. I spoke to his wife, who was American. She didn't seem to know what she really wanted and asked if I had an interior designer working for me. As usual, I said yes, though I didn't even know one. I asked Lou Raines, a friend who was an actor, to stand in and told him to try and persuade her to have magnolia painted over wood chip wallpaper, as I had a load of both that I had bought cheap.

We met with the doctor's wife and Lou pulled out all the stops, being very camp and saying, 'I can see it now: an elegant picture rail that just flows around the room, beautiful Victorian cornices and wooden panels that meet the skirting boards.' I thought he was a bit over the top, but she seemed to think he was the perfect man for the job and asked him to suggest a colour scheme. He went on at length about making up colour boards and how it would take time, acting like he was King Lear. Eventually he said, 'Thinking about it, the only colour I can see working in here is magnolia painted over woodchip paper, Madam.' Oddly enough, she agreed with him. Since it was easier to paint the ceilings the same colour as the walls, Lou suggested that too, telling her that it was all the rage in London and all the fashionable people were having it done. Again, she agreed. I think he could have told her anything and she would have agreed, she was so happy with him.

She readily accepted my quote for the job and gave me a fifty percent deposit upfront, saying that she and her husband were going on holiday and wanted the job finished by the time they got back. That was fortunate because I was able to get Lou to help me without any suspicions about the designer doing the painting as well!

The room was huge and the ceiling very high, so I hired a ten foot ladder. Unfortunately we couldn't get it round the corner out of the hallway and into the room. My next brainwave was to spray paint everything and get the job done quickly and easily. I hired paint sprays and we tried it - pointed them at the ceiling and went for it. Sprays of paint instantly erupted ... and then fell ... like fine rain! We looked at each other, swearing and laughing while it covered the pair of us from head to toe! Being no match for gravity, we had to devise a series of steps and ladders and do it the hard way.

We ended up doing a really nice job. Even though we may have strung the client along a bit, she was delighted when she came back and saw the finished job; she said she would be recommending us to all of her friends.

Lou helped me out on more than one occasion. You only had to say one word to Lou and he would fall in with whatever the situation was. I did not yet have an office, but I knew a man who did – sort of! My friend Ozzie (Oscar to his clients) was an estate agent and he lent me empty flats that were up for rent. It was great when they happened to be furnished, but, mostly, they were unfurnished and I didn't keep anything in them; I just needed them to have an address that gave the company more credibility. And we often had posh ones like Wigmore Street or Portland Place that sounded very good for the business. Ozzie let me know when he had to show them to prospective tenants, and I stayed out of the way. When someone took a flat, obviously, I had to 'move out'.

Lou was with me, one day, when we heard a key in the door and in came Ozzie with a woman. He had forgotten I had the keys! He looked at us and just got flustered, not knowing what to say. I knew I had to think of something. 'We've got a fantastic idea for this place!' I said to him enthusiastically, and then turned to the woman, 'Oh, I'm sorry! Are you interested in the place?' She introduced herself; she was American; I knew I wouldn't have a problem! 'We're contractors,' I told her, 'and we're just looking over the place to see what needs doing or what improvements can be made.' Ozzie relaxed a bit and Lou took over, going on about various ideas. The woman got interested, mentioned some things she'd like done and ended up taking the place on those conditions. We got the job!

As time went on, I managed to get a few contracts, maintaining blocks of flats. Through this, I met an actual interior designer who looked after a block of flats in Kensington, all owned by Arabs. At that time in London there were many Arabs who came over here and spent fortunes. The interior designer introduced me to quite a few of the owners and I would always give her commission at the end of a job.

The flats were enormous – twice the size of mine, and mine was big. The owners would ring up any hour of the day or night with problems, but that did not matter because we started making a lot of money. One person phoned in the middle of one night because the kettle wasn't working and he wanted a cup of tea. I went over, put a fuse in the kettle and he gave me fifty pounds! That might not sound like much now, but it was then. I got so much money in cash, I used to bring it home and we counted it on the bed. It was thousands, and not all of it was from maintenance work, part of it was from selling spare car parts. A very nice Arab I'd done some work for told me that in Saudi Arabia they had trouble getting them, especially for older cars. He asked me to help him find some for Hilman Imps and, as usual, I agreed. Not having a clue where I could get these parts, I decided the best place to start would be the manufacturer. They told me that they did not stock parts for this particular model but they gave me the numbers of some collectors to try. After a couple of phone calls I managed to find a company, Midnight Motors, that could get starter motors and as many spark plugs as I needed.

I told the Arab the good news and then the bad news: I could get the parts but they were extremely expensive. He told me that he didn't care how much they were. Fancy saying that to me! He was very impressed and explained that he and his brother were not on speaking terms. He was going to open up a shop, next to his brother's shop in Saudi Arabia, and sell all the parts that his brother couldn't get, just to annoy him. He did say that he would end up giving all the parts to his brother, when he had finished his little joke. I couldn't believe he was spending all this money on a little joke, but who was I to argue; I was going to make a fair bit out of this.

I arranged for Midnight Motors to have the parts delivered: four crates of starter motors and two crates of spark plugs. There were fifty starter motors in a crate and two thousand spark plugs in the other two crates. I spoke to the Arab and gave him the price. He didn't even blink. If the deal went ahead, I would earn fifteen hundred pounds. The people from Midnight Motors were also going to earn a fair profit. The deal went ahead and the Arab asked me to pick him up and drive him to a Barclays bank; all he had were traveller's cheques and he needed cash. At the time I only had an old yellow post office van and Jeanette didn't think it was a good idea to pick him up in that, but I didn't have a choice. I drove him to the nearest Barclays, and we came back with thousands in cash in that old van.

The interior designer who had introduced us, rang some weeks later and told me that he could not get the parts out of England without a special export licence and would like to talk with me. I rang him and explained that there was nothing I could do. He wanted to know if I thought Midnight Motors would take the parts back. I had to tell him that they wouldn't because it had been a special order. All he said was, 'Never mind!'!

He rang me when he returned to Saudi and asked if I could get hold of JCB's . Again, I didn't have a clue, but the manufacturer told me that they had a factory in Saudi Arabia where they stored machines. As a 'thank you' for the information, the guy sent me five hundred pounds!

One flat owner wanted all his carpets and curtains cleaned. I thought I'd take the curtains to the dry cleaners, but Jeannette said I shouldn't because they were heavy velvet and could shrink, or something else could happen to them. I hired a steam cleaner to do the carpets and a mate of mine, who was a copper and used to come and help me with the decorating sometimes, came to help me do them. That seemed pretty simple, so I decided to steam clean the curtains the same way. They got soaking wet. The woman who looked after the flats came in and said it all smelled nice but she was a bit worried about how wet the curtains were. I told her it was a special process and they would look lovely when they dried.

They didn't dry for about three weeks! And when they did, they'd shrunk by about two feet! Unfortunately, the carpet had shrunk as well! It was coming out of the grippers, like an animal trying to hang on as it slowly lost its grip! I'd used too much water. The woman who looked after the flats was a lovely woman and I managed to talk her round: I told her that we used this process all the time and the curtains and carpets were a load of rubbish. She later rang me and said she'd told the owner all this, and he'd just told her to get rid of them and buy new ones because he hadn't bought them in the first place; they'd come with the flat. I had a mate in the carpet business so I got him in to do the carpets. Unfortunately, I didn't know anyone in the curtain business!

Business was booming when I had a call from a girl called Susannah. She looked after a number of flats owned by Mobil Oil and used by their personnel who came to London and stayed for a few months, and she wanted someone to do general maintenance. To begin with, she asked me to do some estimates for the decorating that was needed. It was only me and whomever I could get to come and help me, but I went and gave the estimates. They were beautiful flats in places like Warwick Square and Eton Square and, within a week, I was decorating one of them.

Susannah was very attractive and living with a very rich man who gave her everything she wanted. When I finished the job and she was paying me, she asked if I would decorate their flat, which was situated in Kensington. I went round and met her boyfriend, Tariq, who showed me all the rooms that they had decided to have decorated. We came to an agreement and I started the following week.

I needed a carpenter and hired a fellow called David, who was recommended by a friend. He was tall and very good looking, and Susannah took to him straight away. Everything seemed to be going well until Tariq called to say he needed to see me straight away. When I got to the flat, he and David were having an argument: Tariq had caught David smoking grass in his flat and wanted him off the job straight away. David looked like he was going to punch Tariq, so I grabbed him and dragged him out of the flat, explaining to him that I would not have this contract put in jeopardy and that he would have to go. He apologized, knowing he had really messed up, and gave me the name of another carpenter, Damien. I went back up to the flat and apologized to Tariq and Susannah, promising that I would sort out the mess.

A couple of weeks after Damien started, Tariq rang and asked me to meet him in a coffee bar just round the corner from the flat, to discuss the rest of the work that needed to be done. He was very pleased with everything and paid me for all that had been done so far, after which we went up to the flat to see how Damien was getting on. We walked in, casually chatting; Tariq pushed the kitchen door open and there was Damien with the maid up against the wall and his trousers round his ankles! Damien looked round in shock. 'Sorry Steve, I didn't have time to sweep up!' he said, trying to lighten the situation. Tariq didn't see the joke and slammed out of the room. I don't know if the maid kept her job, but we managed to the get the work finished without any more carpenter mishaps, and Tariq was very pleased with the outcome.

Susannah had mentioned to me that Mobil Oil was having a Christmas party. Tariq couldn't go and she asked if I would mind going with her. 'Of course not,' I'd said. The party was a very plush affair at the Howard Hotel in central London; all the Mobil Oil executives attended. It was a lovely evening and I got so sloshed that Susannah had to get me a cab. She got in with me, after I insisted she let me be the gentleman and take her home. We arrived at the flat and she couldn't find her key. She rang the doorbell but there was no answer, so she tried again. This time, a third floor window flew open and clothes came flying past my head, landing on the ground next to me. 'If you want him, go and live with him!' Tariq was shouting in a frenzy of anger.

I was so drunk I think I was actually laughing, but Susannah started crying. 'Tariq, let me in! What's wrong?' she wailed.

'Fuck off!' he retorted and closed the window.

We both got back in the taxi. With her clothes bundled into a ball, she went to stay in a hotel for the night. I can't remember getting home but Jeannette told me that I had turned up in a taxi, in which I had thrown up, and she'd had to pay for cleaning, as well as the fare.

Susannah rang me the next morning, asking me to go and see Tariq and tell him there was nothing going on between us. I was hung over and felt terrible. I didn't want to speak, let alone face an angry, suspicious boyfriend, but I went; it was the least I could do for Susannah after all the work she'd put my way. I was prepared for the worst, but it turned out to be a storm in a teacup. I got to the flat to find Tariq quite shamefaced and apologetic, which was the last thing I was expecting. 'I get very jealous,' he explained. 'I love Susannah very much, and I was thinking all evening about the two of you enjoying yourselves together; I just drove myself mad.'

No argument there! We remained friends, though I never did any more work for him.

Susannah later asked me if I knew anybody who would clean the service flats. They were having trouble finding reliable cleaners, didn't want to have to keep on organizing it all and were looking for somebody to take over the contract. Imagine asking me if I knew anybody who would ... ! Of course, I said 'Actually, I do! You're in luck! My wife used to have a cleaning business.' I told Jeannette and she wasn't pleased: she said she didn't want to do 'bloody cleaning'. She came along to a meeting with Mobil Oil, anyway, and got the contract. She went on to form a nice little company, employing eight girls to clean the service flats and change the sheets and towels. Many times, when one of the cleaners hadn't turned up, she had to do it herself. She isn't made for that type of thing, but she always rises to a challenge and just got on with it. Eventually, her company took over the laundering too. She did well: she had her own money, bought a car and worked for Mobil Oil for quite some time.

Around this time, John North came back into my life.

# 12
# Running Parallel

A message was left on my home answer phone: a client, asking me to do a quote for a job at an address in Clifton Road. When I got there, it was a café, and John North was sitting there waiting for me, a pile of strapped books on the table beside him. I was not pleased to see him. Things were going well and I did not want complications.

'Why the fuck do you keep turning up in my life?' I asked.

'I have a job for you. Six hundred pounds in your pocket and it'll only take a week,' he said, knowing what would get my attention.

That was a lot of money; I could not say no.

He explained that there were two people he wanted me to watch. They were renting a house in Queens Park, and apparently printing fake passports and immigration papers. I was born not far from the address he mentioned, so I knew the area well. His regular team had been watching the address for a while and knew that the two men in question were working as labourers on a building site. This was why they needed me for this job: I had experience of how things worked in the building trade and would be able to blend in unnoticed. He talked for about an hour, filling me in on all the details and showing me pictures of the two men. He finished by telling me that they were dangerous and would stop at nothing to avoid being caught.

I stopped in at the building site where they were working and asked at the site office if there was any work. They took my name and phone number and assured me that they would call if anything came up. I went back to my own business until the site manager phoned a week or so later, and asked me if I wanted a painting job, priming new woodwork.

I made arrangements so that I could be away from my business for a week and started at the building site the next day. The canteen was open when I arrived at 7.30am. The usual array of canteen staff was setting everything up for the first influx of workers. The site did not open until eight and I had arrived early so that I would have time to get some gossip, which was usually rife in a site canteen. Unfortunately, it was just the usual complaints about not getting enough money. Looking around, I thought anything they got was too much; the grease was so thick it clung to the cooking equipment like syrup, and even the table legs were thick with grease. I had actually been hungry before I walked into the place, but, after watching them heat congealed fat in burnt pans, I would rather have starved than eat there. I left to find the site manager, who would show me where I was to work.

I painted until the siren sounded for a tea break and then I went for a wander; I needed to find these blokes. There was a large generator humming away, which almost deafened me as I passed it, and I hurriedly climbed over a massive pile of sand to get away from it. Sitting on the other side were the two men I was looking for. I was shocked and stood rooted to the spot for a second. I had not imagined it would be so easy to find them on such a big site. 'Are you ok?' one of them shouted. With a bit of quick thinking, I told them that I suffered with migraines and had suddenly gone dizzy. 'Come and sit down,' he said. I couldn't believe my luck, although I was not about to count my chickens yet.

They were aged between twenty five and thirty five, and far too well dressed for a building site: their overalls were very clean and I figured that they couldn't have been working as labourers for long. We got into the usual chit chat about the work: I asked them how long they had been working as labourers; not very long, they told me; I mentioned that I was a plumber, but couldn't get any plumbing work on this site. They asked me if I was married and I said, 'No, I've only got my prick to feed.' They fell about laughing and, as the siren went off, signalling for us to get back to work, they mentioned about going out for a drink. I just nodded in agreement and left them.

That evening, as I left the site, I decided it would not be a good idea to go to my car as I did not want anyone seeing my number plate. I walked down the hill to the bus stop and as I stood there an old Ford Fiesta pulled up beside me.

'Do you want a lift?' somebody called.

It was the two men and I walked over to the car, saying that I was going for a drink and did they want to come. They looked at each other and nodded, so I climbed in the back and we drove to a local pub. I told them my name and they came back with theirs: Rick and Marty. We had a few drinks and the usual conversation about sex and money. They also told me that this job was just a stopgap until something better came along. They certainly weren't short of money and Rick kept disappearing to the toilet. It was obvious he was on cocaine: his nose was constantly running and he was very jittery. I did not want to stay too long as it was early days yet and it was best to keep things casual. They drove me to Queens Park station where I hung around until I was sure they had gone, and then I rang John to inform him that I had got in with them and that Rick was definitely on coke. He warned me to be careful of him as he already had a conviction for GBH.

I was in the building site canteen on the following Wednesday when Marty came in and told me about a party that was happening that Friday in a wine bar on the Kilburn High Road. The rest of that week went well and on the Friday evening I went home and got ready. I explained to Jeannette that the job was only supposed to last a week but looked like it was going to take longer. I couldn't give her details about it and she was very understanding: not many women let their men go out most evenings without any real explanation.

The bar was crowded and the music deafening. As I couldn't see Rick or Marty anywhere, I was making my way through the throng of people to get to the bar when someone grabbed my arm and asked me what I was doing there and did I have an invite. While he was grabbing my arm and pulling me over to where a big fat bloke was sitting, I was trying to tell him that Rick and Marty had invited me. Taking no notice, he said something into the fat bloke's ear, the fat bloke said something back, and I was promptly kicked out!

As I was walking down the street, Rick shouted to me from across the road. He ran over to join me and when I explained what had happened, he told me not to worry and we went back to the bar. I waited while he went over to the fat bloke, who waved his arms around at first, but then calmed down, and Rick came back to tell me there was no longer a problem. I could not help feeling sorry for him: if they found out why I was really there, he would probably end up inside six feet of concrete.

I met quite a few people that evening - all crooks. Someone called Billy tried to sell me a Rolex watch and I must admit I was tempted. After a while, from the corner of my eye, I saw the fat bloke moving towards me and I tensed up, waiting for trouble.

'Sorry about before!' he said, offering me his hand. 'The little prick forgot to tell me you were coming. I'm Dan.'

'Steve,' I replied, shaking his hand.

'What business are you in, Steve?'

'Plumbing. I'm working on the same building site as Rick and Marty.'

'Marty is no friend to us!' he said, his face reddening with anger. 'I've told Rick to steer clear of him.'

'Why would that be?' I enquired.

'He's a shit!'

When I later asked Rick why Dan did not like Marty, he told me that Marty had decided to do his own thing and was not giving Dan a cut, but would not elaborate further. I assumed it was drugs.

I was back on the site the following Monday, knowing I was going over my time, but there was no option and John would just have to pay me more. Marty was nowhere to be seen and Rick just said he had other business and would not be back. I stuck close to Rick and by the end of that week he was inviting me to his house for Sunday lunch.

I arrived at an average semi-detached house in Hendon with a Jag and a Rover on the drive, both no more than a year old. I rang the bell and was surprised when Dan opened the door. It turned out he was Rick's father.

The house was clean and tidy, a little over the top with a bar in one corner of the room and every wall covered with cheap paintings. Rick came into the room and patted me on the back, saying, 'All right mate?'

We sat down at the dining table and a young woman, whom I judged to be about twenty five, came into the room. She was introduced as Dan's wife, Lee. I was astonished. Dan was about sixty and no oil painting, whereas, she was very attractive, slightly oriental, with a figure any woman would die for and the biggest eyes I had ever seen. I was completely mesmerized by her as she served up a very nice Sunday dinner of duck. Oblivious to the effect it was having on Dan, I monopolized her and could not stop talking to her.

'Steve!' he finally said. 'If you wouldn't mind leaving my wife alone …'

'Oh! I'm sorry,' I said, hearing the annoyance in his voice and realising I was not being too clevr. I could trip myself badly by forgetting why I was there. 'You're a very lucky man, Dan,' I added, smiling enviously, hoping it would stroke his ego.

'If you knew how much she cost me ...' he said in a low, sinister voice, not finishing the sentence. He was red with anger and his words seemed to hang in the air. To say I was embarrassed would be an understatement. Rick started chatting, and, for a while, tried hard to smooth things over, but Dan was getting steadily drunk. He began rambling about his first wife, who had left him for someone else when he had loved her so much. Lee just sat through it all with tears in her eyes. I felt sorry and embarrassed for her.

We stumbled through lunch until, finally, I felt I could leave. Dan was having none of it, however: he ordered me to stay, saying we had some talking to do, and then he abruptly left the room. Seconds later, he shouted from the back garden for me to join him. The first thing that hit my eye when I went out was a large caravan that looked like it had not been used for a very long time: rust was taking over and all four tyres were completely flat. I wondered why he kept it there

'Private word!' he announced as I approached. 'Rick's a good boy, Steve, but he's easily led astray. He doesn't need to work on the building site; I sent him there to learn what real work is. He took that little shit Marty with him, but he's been dealt with now!'

I could only imagine how, as Dan went on to ask me about my family, where I came from and how much I earned. Naturally, I gave him false information.

'Listen, Steve,' he finally said, 'you seem to have a brain. Look after my boy on that site and I'll look after you.'

I felt like I was getting drawn in and I did not much like it. I did not like myself for all the lying and could not help feeling guilty. I was about to ruin his life.

I spoke to John that evening, saying I was fed up and wanted out. He just told me to stop being stupid and to get on with it; I had come so far in such a short time and I was nearly done; besides, he could not put anyone else on the job now. I told him all about the meal and about Lee. He already knew all about her: she was his informant! 'She's only eighteen,' he said. 'Dan bought her from her family for three thousand pounds.'

*So that he could bring her here and treat her like shit?* I thought. 'Does she know about me?' I asked, panic rising at the thought of my cover being blown.

'Yes,' he said, 'but don't worry, she's reliable. We just thought it better that you didn't know.'

Knowing that young girl was trapped in such a horrible situation, I felt I had to continue.

I met Rick in the site canteen the next day. He apologized for his father and I took the opportunity to ask him what his dad actually did for a living. He told me he ran the wine bar and also had a small stationery supply business.

'On the printing side?' I asked.

'Yeah, kind of,' he replied.

'I used to be a printer with my brothers,' I told him.

'You should mention that to Dad.'

We both went to the wine bar that evening. Dan seemed pleased to see me and asked me into his office to have a drink with him. I told him how I used to be in the printing business and that Rick had told me to mention it to him.

'Why would I be interested in that?' He looked at me suspiciously.

'Rick mentioned that you have a stationery supply business.'

'I thought you were a plumber,' he said.

'I am, but I started out in the print trade, working for my brothers.'

Eyebrows raised, he looked thoughtful for a second and then asked me to his house for dinner, saying there may be a way for me to earn extra cash but he could not talk in the wine bar.

I was excited and rang John as soon as I could to tell him the latest news. He said I needed to calm down and that this was good but it was not over yet: I would have to take the next step; I would have to go for dinner wearing a wire.

On the evening of the dinner, I met earlier with a technician who wired me up and told me how to work the equipment, which was a Nagra, a beautiful, handmade, mini reel-to-reel tape recorder, measuring about seven inches by six, originally designed for MOSAD, the Israeli secret service. It was a superb piece of kit and I'd love to own one now. I had it strapped to my back with surgical tape, and then the microphone came up on a wire from the back to the front of my body and into my pocket. We tested that everything was working well, then off I went to Hendon.

It was a warm evening and the recorder, which I switched on as I arrived at the house, felt slightly awkward and cumbersome. Lee opened the door and greeted me with a kiss on the cheek, whispering into my ear to be careful. As I walked into the living room, Rick got up out of his chair. I stuck out my hand in case he patted me on the back, as he had the previous Sunday. I did not want him feeling the recorder. He stared at me for a second, slightly perplexed, since this was not part of our usual greeting, but then shook my hand. 'Hello, mate,' he said.

I was getting hot, not only from the warm weather but also from sheer nervousness, and, obviously, I could not take my jacket off. When Dan came in from another room he was accompanied by a Thai man, whom he introduced as his business partner Nick. Sweat began to drip down my back and the recorder was starting to irritate.

We all sat around the table and Lee brought in some plates. As the door swung open, I could see another young woman, presumably Nick's wife, in the kitchen. It was the most uncomfortable meal of my life. I could sense an atmosphere, and I could tell that Lee had been crying because her big eyes were red and sore looking. She kept glancing at me while we were eating. No business was discussed over the meal; we just chatted as if we were at a normal dinner party. Nick's wife, Mina, who couldn't speak English, just sat and nodded. Rick did not say a word throughout the meal, which made me feel even more awkward.

When the two women started clearing the table, Dan told me to follow him and Nick into the garden. Rick stayed behind. We strolled around, Dan acting like the big lord in his little semi-detached garden. He talked about Marty for a while, saying how pleased he was that Marty was now off the scene, before leading the way to the caravan and telling me that this was where we were going to discuss real business.

It was messy and looked like no one had been in it for a very long time, but Dan unlocked another door into a completely different room. This one was tidy and clean and had a television fixed to the wall; leather chairs surrounded a coffee table, and there was a fully stocked drinks cabinet. Dan poured me a whisky and unlocked a large filing cabinet. My back was itching badly from the tape and I wondered if it was still running. Dan handed me a large wooden box and told me to open it. It was full of printing plates.

'What are these for?' I asked.

'Money!'

The one word I had been waiting for all evening!

'We're paying a fortune for the printing,' he said. 'Stupid, if you can do it.'

'What about the paper?' I said. 'It has to be the proper stuff.'

'Don't worry about that. We can sort it out,' he said dismissively, taking the wooden box from me.

That seemed to be all he was going to say on the matter. He had clearly already made his mind up that I was going to be their printer, and now he wanted to relax and have a drink. He put the box back into the filing cabinet and pulled out videotape, which he put into a VCR. I was thinking of how I could get out of there and check the recorder on my back, when a porno film flashed onto the TV screen. I was horrified: there, in front of my eyes, were Lee and Mina, performing with three men.

Dan seemed very proud. 'Good, isn't she?' he leered.

I had to nod my agreement. Nick just sat and smiled, never taking his eyes from the TV screen.

'If you want one, Nick's your man! He's in the meat trade!' Dan laughed.

I couldn't believe he was referring to Lee and Mina as if they were animals. I sat for as long as I could and then excused myself to go to the toilet.

'Going for a wank?' Dan laughed crudely.

I got to the toilet, took off my shirt and turned round to look at my back in the mirror. It was red and inflamed, with white streaks running all the way down to my belt: the battery from the recorder had leaked and been eating away at my skin. I gingerly removed the recorder, which had stopped running, probably long before. That meant there was no reason for me to stay in this house a minute longer. I needed to get out: my back was in a terrible state and I was sickened by what I had seen. Thinking this, I nearly jumped out of my skin when a knock came at the door. I was very relieved to hear Lee whispering to let her in.

'Just a minute,' I whispered back as I hid the recorder and microphone under the bath and quickly got my shirt back on.

When I opened the door, Lee came in and grabbed my hands. 'You have to help us, Steve!' she urged. 'We need to get away. I am sure you have seen the terrible things they are making us do.'

'I'll do everything I can to help you,' I promised fervently. 'Now go, before we get caught!'

After I washed the sweat off my face and put the recorder in my pocket, I walked back down the garden to the caravan, hearing the laughing and joking coming from inside it. I told Dan that I had to make a move, as I had a few things to do. He asked me to ring him the following day and let him know what I thought of his proposition. I just nodded. I couldn't wait to leave that house.

As soon as I got home, I rang John and filled him in on the situation there.

'Is the recording good? What did you get?' he asked, apparently unmoved by what I had told him.

'I haven't checked it,' I replied quickly. 'But, whatever happens, we have to get those girls out of there!'

'We will, all in good time. We have to sort out the objective first.'

'You don't really give a shit about those girls, do you?'

'The sooner you get the job done, the sooner they can be rescued.'

I put the phone down, irritated by his heartless professionalism and frustrated by the fact that there was nothing more to be done but have a hot shower and go to bed.

The following morning, I met with John and the technician and told them about the battery leaking on my back; they were shocked and apologetic. The technician rewound the tape and plugged the recorder into an amplifier. It did not sound promising, but after a minute it seemed to spring to life and Dan's voice was heard all over the

144

room. We listened for an hour and, unfortunately, it stopped just before he mentioned the plates. John hesitated, just in case it would start up again, and then told me I would have to do it again. I was not pleased, but he said we had to get more evidence on tape and find out where the printing machine was. As soon as I had done that, he would round everyone up, including the girls. That was enough for me: I immediately rang Dan to arrange a meeting, and we taped the conversation.

When I arrived at the house, Dan was there alone, which was good for me: the last thing I needed was distraction, and a one to one conversation would be clearer on the tape. He seemed to be in a dark mood and told me that he was having trouble with 'the slag', that she wouldn't do as she was told and she was realising that western women had a lot more freedom. Obviously, I realised that he was talking about Lee and just nodded agreement, but did not encourage him to carry on.

Eventually, he made me coffee and we got down to business. 'So, you're in!' he announced, as if it was a foregone conclusion.

'I'm interested,' I responded cagily, 'but first I need to know how much I'm going to get out of this deal.'

'Two percent of everything I sell.'

'Three,' I countered, thinking if I agreed straight away it might look suspicious.

'Done!' he said, putting out his hand to shake on it.

'What kind of machine have you got?' I asked, intent on getting the necessary information.

'It's old but the best that money can buy,' he affirmed before going on to talk about the different inks they used and how good the paper was, never once mentioning where the machine was.

'Is the printer here? It's been a while and I'd like to familiarise myself with it,' I coaxed.

'No, it's in the house in Queens Park where Rick lives. He shifts the money for me,' he said at last.

'What's the address?' I asked nonchalantly. 'I've got a few things to do, but I can meet you there later and take a look at it.'

As he gave me what I'd asked for, I silently cheered.

After hurrying home and listening to the tape, I rang John. 'We've got him bang to rights! It's all on tape and I know where the machine is,' I told him. 'I'm supposed to go over there and check it out.'

'Carry on and do that,' he instructed, 'so we can be sure it's there.'

As soon as I walked into the house in Queens Park, I knew there was a printing machine there: I could smell the white spirit and ink; old memories came flooding back. Dan wasn't there and Rick would not let me near the machine until he arrived. We went into the kitchen to wait.

'Why are you working on the building site when you don't need to?' I asked.

'No-one will suspect me of printing fake money while I'm working there will they?' he laughed. 'Besides, my dad thinks hard work will sort out my panic attacks.'

'You have panic attacks?'

'They started when I was in prison.'

'Why did you go to prison?' I asked, although I remembered the GBH conviction John had mentioned.

He looked ashamed. 'Marty was fucking a Thai bird that Nick had brought over to sell. He started beating her, scarred her face, and Nick went mad because he had paid two grand for her and figured he could sell her on for five. With a scar, she was worthless. Nick sent some heavies over and they started beating the shit out of Marty. I couldn't stand by and watch, so I picked up a scaffold pole and nearly killed them. I don't know why I stuck up for Marty, because I hated him for beating the girl. I don't hit women.'

Rick was sweating profusely; telling this story seemed to have taken a lot out of him. I felt sorry for him. He was a weak man, obviously ruled by his sleaze-ball father, but he did not seem to go along with the way the girls were treated: he had been silent during the meal when Lee had looked as if she had been crying; he had not come to the caravan when his father showed the porno film, and now this.

The front door slammed and the time for talk was gone. Dan came into the kitchen. He had clearly been drinking and asked Rick if he had shown me the machine. When Rick replied that he hadn't, Dan said 'good boy', as if he were talking to a dog.

Dan led me through a door that was about three inches thick, with a metal panel top and bottom. As we walked into the room, it was like going back to my printing days: an old Heidelberg printing machine took centre stage, and makeshift shelves haphazardly lined the walls. Dan asked me if I wanted to try out the machine. I knew he was testing me, to see if I really did know about printing. He switched it on and the fan wheel started to spin. I pushed out the main drive lever and pulled out the impression lever, telling him that the impression lever should never be left pushed in. The look on his face told me that I now had him in the palm of my hand.

He showed me where he stored the paper and the ink. 'You can start tomorrow,' he grinned, pleased as punch.

'I'll see what I can do and call you,' I said, knowing I needed time to find out when John was going to raid the house.

'I'll be waiting,' said Dan.

I rang John as soon as I left and he said they would not leave it any longer, as we now had all the evidence we needed. The next evening, the police raided the Queens Park and Hendon addresses at the same time, arrests were made and John assured me that they would all receive long prison sentences. Except Nick - they never did manage to find him.

John was true to his word and the two girls were sent back to their families in Thailand.

# 13
# A Roller Coaster Ride

I went straight back into my building business but, in all honesty, I was getting disillusioned with the trade and only carried on because the money was good. Maybe it had something to do with the excitement of undercover surveillance work, which I seemed good at - a realisation I owe to John North.

Life was up and down and sometimes we struggled, but we always managed to pay the mortgage and keep going. Then, while we were painting the hallways in a block of flats in Olympia, a guy from a company called Diverse Productions came and asked me to give a quote on some work in an empty building across the road; the company hadn't moved in yet, but was going to. It was just at the time Channel 4 was coming to fruition and starting up, and Diverse Productions wanted painting, electrics, false floors, sound-proofing – a studio, in fact - because they would be recording for Channel 4. Grayson Home Services didn't do the specialised computer connections, but we did everything else and it was a very big job for us; we saw it through to when they started recording.

One day, I got a call about a painting and decorating job at Abbey Road Studios. I put in a tender and got it, which was great because it was such a prominent, well-known building. We had to paint the outside first, and I got a mate to put up scaffolding and had a big banner made to go across the top with *Graysons Home Services* on it.

The scaffolding wasn't very good and we had to keep checking it. I'd had to drop the price right down to get the job, so I couldn't afford anything better. The guy who did it had not been in business long and didn't have enough poles, so we were always waiting for him to go off and find more so we could get a lift up to the next level. I don't know where he got them, but they all had different coloured marks (companies used a certain colour to identify their equipment) and it was like a harlequin parade by the time he finished!

Opposite, there was a block of mansion flats. Somebody came over and asked for a quote to do some painting for him there. He was Arabic and he didn't just want painting: he wanted new central heating and walls taken down; basically it meant gutting the place. He asked me if I could do it and, of course, I said I could, although it was a massive job - the biggest I'd ever done, apart from Diverse Studios. He was on the second floor, and, to knock the wall down, girders would have to be put across the ceiling, down through the floor and the flat underneath, to support the building. I was still working on Abbey Road and I'd have to get in seven or eight people to do this job, but I just didn't have the money to pay them. I shouldn't have taken it on, but I did because it was worth about twenty five thousand pounds. Fortunately, I managed to get fifty percent up front from the owner before we started.

We couldn't move too fast on the new job because I was juggling the money, partly funding the Abbey Road job with it. I had to, because even though we were doing a fantastic job for them and they were very happy with us, a big company like that doesn't pay anything out until the job is finished. In the meantime, the Arabic owner was coming in once a week, always on the same day, to see how we were getting on, and he'd complain because we hadn't got enough done. I'd tell him he couldn't see what had been done under the floor, or whatever, but we were always screaming and shouting at one another; there was an argument every week.

I had a great painter working for me - a young fellow, very thin and lanky, with long blonde hair – and, one week, out of the corner of my eye, I saw him come into the room and creep across behind the owner. I burst out laughing because he was naked underneath a builder's sack that he'd cut holes in for his arms and legs. I couldn't tell the owner what I was laughing at because he'd have thought we were a bunch of clowns, so I covered it up by shouting to the guys to make us a cup of tea. They called us when it was ready, and we went into the other room where I caught the eye of one of the guys and he glanced at the ceiling. Automatically, I looked up. The painter had gone wild with a glue gun! Glue guns had just come on the market then and they were fabulous: they would sick anything to anything. He'd stuck a shovel and everybody's work boots to the ceiling! They were all laughing themselves silly, and I was doing my best not to. The owner was wanting to know the joke. I was on pins in case he looked up before I got him out of the room, but I managed it.

It was hand to mouth all the time. I had to hire another plumber, but I didn't have enough money to pay him. Abbey Road still wasn't finished, and we had got very behind with everything because of continually juggling money, so I had to think of something. I told the Arabic guy that we were getting on so well that I'd arranged to get a quote for the carpets. He thought it was far too early to order carpets because the place was a mess, but I persuaded him that he had to order them then because it would takes ages for them to arrive. I called my mate, who was in the carpet business and still is, and he came round, sorted out the order and I got enough commission to pay the plumber. And that's how it was, all the time.

I couldn't handle the construction work on my own, so I got Dick Briggs, a builder I knew, to come in and do it. He was a really big guy who could drink anyone under the table, and he started knocking the walls down. All of a sudden, a building inspector came, said the people underneath were complaining, and asked for our letter of approval from the council. We didn't have one! Not surprisingly, he made a fuss but it could have been a lot worse. He turned out to be a decent fellow and told us what we had to do and what weight girders we needed and so on. We had nothing to do with it after that because Dick and his mates were taking care of it. It all looked good when they'd finished until my very good friend John, the electrician who was working with me, called me over and pointed out that the bolts holding the girders to the wall were all loose and could be pulled out. There were a lot of them and we tried to tighten them up; they just kept on turning though, because the cement in the walls was so old there was no purchase. In a panic, I called Dick and he came immediately, even though he knew he couldn't fix it. We had to do *something* because the inspector was coming back in a couple of days, plus we were a bit worried about the building coming down! The girders would hold everything, but we still had to sort it out. We were all panicking! We went to a builders' merchant and asked his advice. He suggested this new device that pumped a substance into the wall; this substance then expanded and solidified. It was very expensive but we couldn't afford not to take it. Fortunately it worked and the building is still standing!

During this time, through the carpenters I had hired, I met Glen, a meticulous carpenter of the old school, and we struck up a friendship. He came from Norfolk and shared a flat with three Romany friends, who lived in Norfolk and worked in London during the week. They had their own language and I learned some of it because it came in very handy if we wanted to say something we didn't want anyone else to understand.

After the job opposite Abbey Road Studios finished, I was so busy I decided to take a partner into the business to help me out. I was learning as I went along, and I figured it would be good to have a real tradesman working with me. Glenn seemed the obvious choice, at the time.

We decided that we needed a proper office, as we couldn't keep working from the flats I borrowed from Ozzie. There was an office space going in Maida Vale, close to where I lived. It needed quite a lot of renovation so we decided to get a carpenter in to start work. We had so much money coming in left, right and centre that doing the work ourselves didn't even occur to us.

We advertised in the *Evening Standard* for a general carpenter, and, after seeing two or three blokes whom we didn't like, we had a phone call from a girl saying that her dad would be able to do the job. He came the next morning and stood in front of Glenn and me with a blue metal toolbox that a mechanic would carry, but it was *not* what a carpenter would carry. I could see Glen wasn't impressed. I asked the guy his name and he mumbled something I couldn't make out; he mumbled again and pulled out a piece of paper. On it was written: 'My name is Wally and I am deaf and dumb.' At first, I thought someone was pulling our leg, but we tried to interview him anyway, which was difficult because he could speak but he couldn't hear, so he wasn't intelligible. He tried to write bits of things down and, in the end, I felt sorry for him and offered him a week's trial. He wanted to start right then, and we had all the timber, so we agreed. He turned out to be one of the best carpenters ever; he did outstanding work, and once he had the job he left the silly tin toolbox and brought all his good tools. After a time, I got so used to the way he spoke I could understand him. The only trouble was, no one else could, so we could never send him to a job on his own. But he was fantastic and he was with us for years.

We also took on another carpenter, Alan, whom I mention because he was with me on a job when another situation arose in a dentist's surgery. It was not as catastrophic as the first time with Jimmy

Eat, but it was funny. We got a call out to a major leak and Alan came with me. I had to get up through a hatch into the loft to get to the tank, and the hatch was in the hall outside a dentist's office. I got up there and closed the hatch to stop any dust or dirt coming down into the hall. Alan went to switch the water off and was then waiting to help me down. After I fixed the pipe work, I called to him and he answered, so I just opened the hatch and swung down. I should have looked beforehand, because he wasn't there. I was hanging inches away from the dentist, and over the chair where he was checking somebody's teeth! I hadn't realised there was more than one hatch, and I'd opened the wrong one! Alan came in and was laughing so much he had trouble helping me down; he just couldn't stop. Fortunately, no damage was done, and the dentist and his patient also saw the funny side.

Work kept coming thick and fast, and both Glenn and I bought massive new cars. Lunchtime in the office was a heady mixture of cigarettes and booze, and this often carried on all afternoon. Drinking for most of the day started to take hold of me. I remember Laura being in the office one afternoon, and she found a bottle of Jim Beam whisky in a filing cabinet. Jim Beam was my drink of choice.

By then, Graysons Home Services had been going for a long time, and I should have kept the name, but Glen suggested we change it. He had already had a company called Glennings Limited, which had gone bankrupt, and enough time had elapsed that he could set up again. A limited company meant limited liability for debts, which would be safer, in theory, if anything went wrong;

Graysons became Glennings London Limited. Why I went along with that when he had already gone bankrupt once, I don't know. The drink had befuddled my brain.

We got more work at Abbey Road. I was still known there and as we'd done a good job of painting the outside, they asked us to do all the floors. The bar had been altered, but it was still very cheap to drink there. I was in my heaven and my drinking just got worse and worse. Every night, I would pitch up at the bar and stay there, drinking with Meatloaf or whoever was there, until it closed. At Christmas time, we decided to have a party there and invited everyone we knew. A scaffolding contractor gave us a present: not a bottle of whisky, but six grams of cocaine, so off we would trot every so often to the toilets and shove it up our noses; there were more people in the toilets than there were at the party!

I never thought much about drinking and driving in those days and, by some strange chance, I never got caught. Fortunately for me, and everyone else, I didn't have any accidents either, except for the time I woke up in the car after passing out and driving into the central barrier. No one was there, the police hadn't spotted me, and I just drove home. I took Laura to school every morning, and that morning, when she went out and got in the car to wait for me, she found flowers all over the back seat. To this day, I don't know how they got there.

I was spending a lot of time away from my family, neglecting them without realizing it, until one day, when I rolled in drunk, Jeannette told me if I wanted to live the single life and go out drinking with my mates, I should leave. My bags were packed and waiting on the landing for me. I decided to humour her, stay a few nights at Glen's flat and see what happened. That's how cavalier I was about it! Unbelievable!

It was only a two bedroom flat; there was hardly enough room for them, let alone me as well. It was also none too clean and smelled of sweaty feet, greasy take-aways and cigarettes. My first night there, dinner was a fried chicken take-away, with the leftovers kept for the next day's breakfast. I thought I was 'jack the lad', on my own again and getting pissed with the boys. It was a game, a novelty. Apart from getting drunk every lunchtime and evening, our main entertainment, every morning, was looking through binoculars at the woman over the road, stripping off to get into her bath. We would fight over the binoculars like a bunch of schoolboys in the playground, and I soon realised how ridiculous it all was.

I was not used to sharing a bed with filthy, smelly builders, either, and having a bath in the same water as four other men, a situation which came about because there was no sink. One of the guys had come home drunk, tried to pee in it, leant on it and broken it. Everywhere was flooded, including the flat below. There we were, five builders, and not one of us thought to turn the water off! That left the bath to wash in and only an Ascot water heater, which didn't provide enough hot water for separate baths, so everyone used the same bath water. I was the last one to move in, so I was the last one in the bath. I literally had to break the scum apart to get in. It was just disgusting. I was in and out very fast.

I soon wanted to go back home. When I tried, however, it became clear that Jeannette did not want me back. She's not a person who needs to have someone around her all the time; she loves her own space. I kept ringing and pleading with her, but she was enjoying her new life without me, which was a very big wake-up call for me. I thought I had made a complete mess of things *again*, and she would never have me back. I wouldn't give up though, and I also wanted to see Laura, so I kept on ringing until, finally, after a few weeks, she agreed to bring Laura and meet me at a hotel for lunch.

Laura came running up to me, shouting, 'I really miss you, Daddy!' That really upset me and I thought, *what am I doing?* Jeannette was very cold and hard, as she could be then. She's a very strong, good woman who doesn't lie, doesn't suffer fools gladly and says it like it is, which is probably why we're still together. She's mellowed over the years, maybe because she's had to, but I really do not know how she has stuck with me. It was a very uneasy lunch that day, but she did say she would think about having me back.

A few days later, she agreed, on the understanding that things would change, and if they didn't she would want a divorce. Obviously, I had to cut right down on the drinking and stop the Jim Beam altogether, because she said it made me nasty.

I was so elated that I treated her to a few days at a health farm and then, while she was away, I knocked walls down and made a new kitchen. All my mates helped me and we redecorated every room in the house, put in new lights, new carpets, everything was brand new for when she came home, and the bedroom was like something out of *House and Garden*; it was fabulous. When she walked in, I waited for her to notice. And waited! She was so tired she just went to bed and then, as she lay down, she said, 'Is that a new lampshade?'!

My father collapsed from a brain aneurysm in November of that year, and did not regain consciousness before he died two weeks later. He was eighty years old, and, after many hard years, he and my mum had enjoyed some easier years together. They had looked after us, and then we looked after them, making sure they were comfortable. But Mum always did everything for Dad, too much so sometimes, it seemed to us, but I think that's generally how it was for that generation: the husband went out and earned the money, and the wife looked after him. He was not very independent and would have been lost if he had had to go out and buy a suit by himself, or cook a meal. My mum would not have it any other way, even on the day of his death. We were all at the hospital and Mum was washing my unconscious dad. My sisters wanted her to leave him alone, but she wouldn't, she couldn't; she looked after him as she had always done, right up to the last hours. It was twenty six years ago, but I cannot think of those moments without getting emotional.

At Glennings London Limited, work kept coming, and the business did well for several more years before it turned, in 1985, and began to gather momentum on the downward slope.

Hindsight is easy, but I can now see I should have been satisfied with staying a one-man-band, but it all seemed so easy. Everything I touched had worked and I wanted to go that one step further, make it better, aim for the whole nine yards. It was a mistake. I should never have taken on a partner and expanded, poured thousands into renovating an office suite and taken on staff. Glen and I did not work the same way: I wasn't too proud to go out and work with my hands and do whatever was necessary; he always wanted to pay to get someone in. He was very skilled and good with the men, but he was lazy and he didn't have the 'go' that I had. I'm not saying it was all his fault when things began to go wrong; it wasn't. There were a lot of factors, not least drinking, and we were both to blame.

Cash flow became such a problem that, although we had the work, we could not afford to do it, and, for a while, it seemed fortunate that we were on friendly terms with the bank manager. When I was working on Diverse Productions, I had opened an account with a bank close by. The job had taken months, during which time I got to know the bank manager. Those were the days when you could actually see one! He was a really nice fellow and Glen and I had kept the account there. Now, he would ring up and say our overdraft was getting ridiculous; we would take him out for a drink and the three of us would get pissed out of our heads. He liked us and he used to say he didn't know how I got away with being so cheeky. And then he'd sign off on the overdraft! He did not do us any favours. It seemed like he did at the time, but actually, we just kept getting deeper into debt. In the end, we had to let people go and, eventually, the phones stopped ringing and the work just dried up.

Glennings London Limited ended up owing sixty thousand pounds, which was a *lot* of money in the eighties, and we had to go bankrupt. It was very sad. I had started the company and built it up from nothing on my own. It wasn't easy to see it all disappear.

We went to the bankruptcy hearing expecting all the creditors to be there and dreading the discussion about what we owed and how we were going to pay it back. It was in a building behind Paddington Station. There was a top table with an adjudicator sitting there, somebody from the bank and ... nobody else. I kept waiting for the rest to show up, two companies in particular – suppliers – we had been expecting. They had sent letter after letter beforehand, chasing us for the money we owed them. This was their chance, yet nobody turned up, which meant the debts were written off and they got nothing. It did not make any sense.

'You're going to buy your car back, aren't you, Mr Grayson?' my solicitor asked, towards the end of the proceedings, just to add to my confusion. This was a big BMW that had cost nine thousand pounds.

'I will when I get the money,' I replied.

'You can buy it back for five hundred pounds,' he said. 'Is that agreeable to everyone?'

Well, there was nobody there to disagree! I didn't understand what was going on.

We went out for a drink afterwards and got plastered, which was the easy bit! We met up with the guy who had done the scaffolding for us at Abbey Road. He was a rogue, but he'd built a successful company, partly on the start I had given him back then, and he had come a few times to see us and wish us well while all this was going on.

'Sorted for you?' he said mysteriously, smiling into his whisky. 'They won't be bothering you again.'

No matter how much I pressed him for answers, he would not say another word on the subject. All I knew was that he had done us a big favour: somehow, he had got to the suppliers! How he had done it, or what had been said, I still don't know.

Although we were both bankrupt, Glen had nothing for them to take except a little property in Norfolk that wasn't worth tuppence at the time. He got off scot-free and started another business, taking all my contacts, while the bank went after me for the fifty thousand pound overdraft; although I didn't have the money, I had the equity. Jeannette and I had a meeting with them and agreed that we had to sell the flat. That was easy. It was a huge flat and we had made it beautiful; we accepted an offer on it the first day we put it on the market, which kept the bank quiet, but then we had to find the money to keep on paying the mortgage until the sale went through.

It was a terrible low point. I don't have the words to say how traumatic it was. I was taking tranquillisers because of the state I was in, and I was also having terrible migraines. The pain was so bad I wanted to shoot myself. I just did not know *what* to do. We still had people ringing us up for money: suppliers or people who had done work for us. John, the electrician, was good enough to waive what we owed him after I'd paid as much as I could, but others kept after me.

After I'd sold everything I had, I needed money badly and I was desperate. Without telling Jeannette, I took all her jewellery and pawned it.

I knew she would be upset but I didn't think she would mind too much because it was not the first time I had pawned her jewellery. In our early days together, when I was doing a bit of wheeling and dealing and needed some money badly, she had given me a beautiful interlocking wedding and engagement ring, which she had from her first marriage, and told me to get as much for it as I could. It had been made in Switzerland and had a beautiful diamond in the middle; the design was gorgeous. I took it down to the pub and said I'd bought it from some fellow, but, of course, they thought it was stolen so I only got fifty quid for it. When I got home and told Jeannette, she cried. I'll never forget that. Naturally, I promised her I would buy her a better one. And I did; I bought her a lot, which, amongst other things, I was now pawning. I should have asked, but I couldn't take the risk of her refusing.

Everybody wanted to help, but whatever they were giving me was like a drop in the bucket and I was at the end of my tether. I had all this money to pay back for Glen as well as myself, look after my family, pay the mortgage and all the rest that goes with living. It was just me, on my own, and I did not know what else to do. I'm not proud that I pawned my wife's jewellery, but I'm not ashamed either. What's the stuff for, anyway? It was there and we needed money. What good is wearing a load of jewellery if you have nothing to eat? I did intend to buy it back when I could, but her mother got it back for her before that happened. Jeannette's parents

163

were always very good to us. Jeannette now has a beautiful five-diamond ring, which I've since given her and never pawned!

I would have done anything to make money, but I never ever broke the law. I probably would have if I ever got the chance, but, fortunately, I never did. I tried to get a job as a plumber but could only get one as a painter. I stayed with it for a while, even though I was getting peanuts, because it kept us going. I was also selling bolts of fabric for someone I knew who was going bankrupt and had a warehouse that he said he was going to burn down for the insurance money. I thought he was joking, but he wasn't! I didn't know that, though, when I agreed to help him sell this cloth to little shops, and I made a bit of money, which also helped us to live.

Money was not all that was worrying me. My mother was in hospital; she had cancer. We had been going to see her regularly and her spirits were good, so much so that they were talking about discharging her, which didn't seem right to me. I had the feeling she was a burden to them and she was taking up a bed.

Without any warning, the hospital rang up, one day, and said we should go in immediately because she would not live much longer. I couldn't believe it. She had been laughing, joking and reading when I had last seen her. I had asked her, then, if she was in any pain and she had said she wasn't because she was on a morphine drip. When I got to the hospital, only two days later, she was lying there, obviously heavily drugged. She didn't recognise me right away, and she was so drugged she was struggling to talk. It upset me and I cried, which I don't often do. I lay on the bed with her and she managed to ask where Sam and Ray were; she wanted to see her family before she died. Those were her last words to me.

Sam and Ray had not come to the hospital, but I understood that: everybody has their limits and they were just not able to see Mum like that. What I could not accept was what I thought the hospital had done. I went to one of the nurses, very angry, and accused the hospital of putting too much morphine into her, saying that my mother didn't die quickly enough for them and they'd killed her. My sisters had seemed so hard, saying that Mum was dying and that was the end of it, and then the nurse said the same thing: 'Mr Grayson, she was dying anyway.' In the state I was in, that just confirmed it for me. Admittedly, she was dying anyway, but I was convinced she had died of a morphine overdose. It was probably my grief talking then, but I still have my doubts.

She was here one minute and then she was gone. I thought of all those years when she had worked so hard to bring us up; her whole life had been her family, and now it was over. She even managed to leave us one hundred pounds each. That upset me too. She must have been saving for years to do that and gone without herself; whether we needed it or not, she just wanted to give it. She was a fantastic woman.

It was a bad time all round, until, finally, things took a turn for the better when I got a plumbing job. It was way out of my league - all specialised central heating, which I had never done - but I had to take the job. I also got a job there for Dick Briggs, who was out of work at the time (probably a few houses had fallen down!). He was pretty useless at the job – we both were - but he would cover for me when I had a migraine and couldn't work. He had cancer of the mouth, so there were days when he couldn't come in to work, and then I'd cover for him: we helped each other. The migraines got so bad that I got hold of some phenobarbital, which was superb for getting rid of the pain. I was careful not to take it unless I really had to though, because it's so addictive. Eventually, the migraines tailed off and I was able to get stuck into the work. I didn't do a bad job of it either.

After a while, Dick left and started up a business again. He got a big contract and asked me if I wanted to work for him, so I did. Once a week, the guys all met at the Warrington in Maida Vale, a pub well known to Londoners because Lily Langtree had had a flat above it, where she used to meet the king. We met there because that was Dick's 'office'. He would have a bottle of champagne in an ice bucket next to all of us in our dirty clothes, and he would be drinking that while we were drinking beer; he was up and I was down! He would sit there and dole out everyone's wages in cash: a thousand here, a thousand there, five hundred for somebody else, and so on. He only ever dealt in cash – bundles of it! He knew I could sell, so I would sometimes go with him and help get a job, which also gave me a little extra money here and there. He was good to me, like I was good to him when he was down.

That was all very well, but I needed more in my life. I remembered Nickos, a Greek whom I had met at Abbey Road Studios. He had been living here for over twenty years and was a freelance photographer in the newspaper industry. I still had his phone number and I decided to give him a ring. I explained my situation, told him I could develop films and take pictures and asked if he would help me get started in his profession. 'You need a lot of nerve, Steve,' he said. Well, I had plenty of that! After working for John North, nothing fazed me, definitely not taking pictures of stars and celebrities.

He took me to various receptions and award ceremonies; anywhere he knew there would be celebrities. I noticed that the other photographers at the events all stood together, shoving, arguing and jostling for position to take a picture. I could not understand it; I decided this would be an ideal job for me because I knew I could do better. I had had training from an expert in interrogation and surveillance and I knew how to get results. After two or three weeks of shadowing Nickos, I decided to go out on my own.

Nickos told me all the important events were listed in Press newspapers, and from there I could decide where to go.

On my maiden outing alone, I went to a reception Paul McCartney was giving at the Dorchester to publicise a new album he was releasing. I could see at least forty photographers at the door, again all jostling for position as Paul made his entrance. I went off to the side, away from the photographers, and when Paul came to a stop I called out to him. He turned, spotted me and came over, saying, 'Bloody hell! How are you? Are you with this crowd?'

I was pleased that he remembered me from Abbey Road, but I remembered to quickly take some pictures before I replied. 'Yes I am, at the moment,' I then said, moving out of the way to let the other photographers, who had followed him over to me, get their pictures.

'See you later?' asked Paul as he waved and disappeared into the Dorchester.

I nodded, sitting on my laurels, enjoying the fact that I had the best pictures of the night and not taking the obvious next step. While most of the photographers left to go back to their various newspapers, and I should have been taking my pictures straight to a newspaper and selling them, I hung around at the reception having a great time. The next day the pictures that came out in various national papers were all the same and very boring. I had missed a really good opportunity.

I carried on working for Dick, but I always carried a camera with me just in case something happened, and, after work, I would stroll around taking pictures of anything that caught my eye, then go home and develop the films. At the weekends, I went down to Kings Cross and took pictures of prostitutes standing on the corners with their pimps, and I also found that pictures of tramps came out well. I practised and practised my picture taking techniques because I was determined to be good, and I kept on developing films until I could do it efficiently and quickly. The way I had done it before was in a controlled environment and I could take my time; in the newspaper business you didn't have time.

# 14
# Picture It

I looked in the trade magazines every week to find out what was going on, although there were a lot of events I could not get into because I did not have a proper Press Pass. I had applied for one, but they are issued by the Metropolitan Police and it was taking such a long time that I began to worry about my record. Was the crime against Austin Reed and my subsequent conviction coming back to haunt me?

In the meantime, I took any photography job I could get, however strange. On one occasion, Ronnie, a gay photographer I had met at Abbey Road, rang and asked me to meet him for a drink at the Vauxhall Tavern to talk about a possible job. I had not been there in years so, when I walked through the massive wooden and glass doors, I was surprised to find that it looked just the same. It was absolutely packed, although now there were more girls, obviously lesbians.

I pushed my way through the crowd to get to the bar, and stood with my pint of bitter, feeling like everybody was looking at the straight guy. I was beginning to wonder if Ronnie was going to turn up when he shouted from the other side of the bar and beckoned me over. He was with two other guys whom he introduced as Bryan and Andrew. We tried to talk pleasantries over the music, but it was giving me a sore throat so we left and got a cab, which Ronnie directed to the Black Horse, a boxy, modern pub that didn't look very exciting, but I didn't care as long as it was quiet.

Ronnie explained that the job he had called me about was taking pictures at a party Bryan and Andrew were planning. They were obviously a couple because they could not keep their hands off each other - not that that bothered me, especially since I would earn two hundred pounds for the evening.

Bryan opened the door of their lovely detached house dressed in a see through cheesecloth suit. My embarrassment on seeing him was made all the worse by the fact that my red face just seemed to turn him on. The interior of the house was sumptuous: there were chandeliers that would have looked at home in the Albert Hall, and a lot of over the top French pre-revolutionary style furniture.

'Hi Steve, glad you could make it,' called Andrew from the top of a small staircase.

I looked up to see him dressed quite normally, if you can call a cat suit normal! He looked as if he had thirty pounds worth of change down the front of his pants!

Just after 10pm, the guests started to arrive - a couple of girls but mostly men – and the party got underway. For a couple of hours, I took pictures of everyone enjoying themselves. I noticed that Bryan and Andrew seemed to be missing but I just carried on. Suddenly, the lights dimmed and the weirdest music started to play: a sound I can only describe as a cross between nineteen twenties music and electronic. I saw someone coming down the stairs dressed in a tight fitting fur outfit and a frightening headdress with large twisted horns springing from it. It looked like foam was coming from its mouth, which made the hairs on the back of my neck stand up. I could not take a picture; I could only stare. Andrew followed closely behind dressed as a woman with a powdered wig, powdered face and rosy-red painted cheeks. The guests from the party moved away and formed a circle.

All I can say is that what went on in the next hour was the most bizarre thing I have ever seen and most probably ever will. Andrew bent over, lifted his dress, and one of the guests stepped from the circle and pretended to mount him, much to the delight of whoever was in the fur suit. I continued to stare until one of the other guests reminded me to take pictures, as that was what I was there for. I took frame after frame as different people enjoyed themselves with Andrew.

After an hour, the circle re-formed with the weirdo in the suit and Andrew in the middle. Everyone started to chant, at which point I really wanted to get out! Bryan appeared dressed in a cloak with a moon and stars on it, and on his head sat a large crown, which surprised me because I had thought all along that he was in the fur suit. Andrew and the fur suited person lay flat on the floor in front of Bryan, who pulled out a large knife with a slightly curved tip. My stomach turned as he made stabbing gestures towards the strange creature on the floor. The knife was dripping with blood, although it had never made contact. Bryan pulled the knife across the creature's throat and the blood seemed to drip much faster; then, he knelt down and pulled the headdress off the creature. There was Ronnie, sweating profusely and looking as white as a sheet while the people in the circle chanted, 'SHAME, SHAME, SHAME', at the same time pretending to kick him before dispersing.

Ten minutes later, normal music was playing again and everyone was having a good time at the party. Andrew, Ronnie and Bryan came back downstairs dressed normally ... well, depending on what you call normal!

I had to ask what that had been about! Evidently, it was a fifteenth century witchcraft cleansing ritual, performed when someone was unfaithful. Apparently, Ronnie and Andrew had been having an affair, and Bryan had found out. Why they couldn't have bought Bryan some flowers and taken him out for a meal, I don't know! But it all turned out well: Bryan and Andrew went on to open a restaurant in the East End and Ronnie carried on as a photographer. Oh, and the blood I had seen on the knife was fake.

Some of those jobs paid good money but my goal was the newspaper business and I was both nervous and pleased when I was finally called for an interview with the police. All went well and I got my first Press Pass. I walked out of the police station thinking, *this is the beginning of my new life!*

I read in *Melody Maker* that Whitney Houston was due to perform at Wembley Stadium the following night. I needed a Photo Pass to get in and I knew it was a long shot at such short notice but I found out who the agent was and rang up.

'Hi, my name is Steve Grayson. I'm a freelance photographer who specializes in concert photographs for newspapers and magazines,' I announced confidently.

'Yes?' said the secretary, after which there was a long silence.

'Are you still there?' I asked.

'Yes.'

'My name is Steve Grayson ...'

'I heard you the first time.'

That made my blood boil, but I bit my lip. 'I'm trying to get a Photo Pass for the Whitney Houston concert tomorrow.'

'Do you know how many people have called me today, trying to get a Photo Pass for that concert?' she shouted.

'No, but I'm sure your going to tell me!' I said sarcastically while thinking, *what a bad tempered bitch.*

She slammed down the phone.

I gave it half an hour and rang back. 'Good afternoon,' I said pleasantly. 'I'm ringing on behalf of Picture News. I'm very sorry to bother you, but my secretary has just informed me that she's forgotten to write to you as we normally do. Could we possibly have a Photo Pass for tomorrow night's concert?'

She kept me waiting for a short while and then came back, saying she couldn't find a record of us in her files.

'That's unbelievable!' I exclaimed. 'We handle 50% of syndication.'

'I'm sorry,' she apologized. 'Could I have your number and ring you back?'

I gave her my home number, told her to ask for Alan and, if I wasn't there, to give the message to my secretary. I then thanked her, very politely, for her help.

Within the hour she called back, apologizing for the delay and saying she would leave a Photo Pass at the box office the following afternoon. She finished by telling me to mention her name, Sylvia. I told her she had a beautiful name and thanked her for her help!

It was my first concert as a photographer and I was really excited. I arrived early at the box office to pick up my pass. Already there were crowds of photographers milling around the stage door, taking out their cameras and checking their lenses. I could not help noticing that they all had two or three cameras with an assortment of lenses. I only had one camera and two lenses, one of which was so long you could have seen a fly on a tree, the other so short that to get a decent picture I would have to be standing on top of Whitney. However, that was all I had and it would have to do. I stood next to an older photographer, watched his every move and copied everything he did.

The band started up and the audience erupted with excitement; the noise was deafening. Whitney walked out on stage like a queen to her throne. She looked fabulous, wearing a pair of high heels any woman would die for and a long flowing white dress studded with rhinestones. I was enjoying the spectacle so much I didn't realise the other photographers were clicking away and had already taken a roll of film before I had even started. First rule of the job: do not get involved in what is going on around you; just take the pictures you are there to get!

I lifted the camera and looked through the viewfinder: I could see every flaw in Whitney's face; the only way I was going to get a decent picture of her was to go across the road and take it from there. I attached my other lens. Now she was too far away. Christ! I had mucked up already! If only I had taken a picture as she walked across from the other side of the stage, instead of being engrossed in watching the proceedings.

Another photographer tapped me on the shoulder. 'We all have to start somewhere!' he said, offering me another lens to try. I attached it to my camera and it was perfect. I took a whole roll of film. After the concert, we went to a nearby pub for a drink and a chat, and when it was time to leave, he moved forward as if he was going to kiss me on both cheeks. Not thinking anything of it and assuming he was continental, I kissed *him* on both cheeks. As it turned out, all he had wanted to do was talk into my ear because the music was so loud. He just smiled about it, but I felt like a right prat! Jeannette and I still laugh about that incident. I won't forget him, anyway, because there were not many photographers who would help someone out like that - too much competition.

I was so excited with the film I had shot that I rushed home and developed it. It was fantastic and I still have one of the prints on the wall in my house. Fantastic it might have been, but I still didn't earn any money from it. Again, I was too late. I had to get used to deadlines!

Looking in the trade magazines again, I found that there was a reception for the best-dressed man with a tie being held at the Savoy. Yes, the best dressed man with a tie! I decided to go along just to get some experience.

I arrived at the Savoy, showed my Press Pass and was directed to a very large room with tables already laid out with food and drink. I must have been about an hour late because it seemed quite full and I could see a lot of celebrities, Sir John Gielgud amongst them. Sir John recognised me and asked how I was. We chatted for a while until I told him, somewhat reluctantly, that I needed to circulate, as I was there to work. Looking around, I spotted Norman Wisdom standing next to a window. I went over and asked him if I could take a picture. He nodded, turned his hat sideways and pulled his usual Norman Wisdom face. Although the pictures were great, I didn't care whether I could sell them or not: I just wanted all the experience I could get because I was determined to be the best, whatever happened.

One of the photographers that I met that evening told me about a big event taking place at the Criterion Theatre in Piccadilly the coming Saturday - something to do with Red Nose Day. John, my electrician friend, came with me. Quite a lot of celebrities turned up: Billy Connolly and Lenny Henry amongst many others. The press photographers were there, jostling, as usual. I just stood back and watched them. It was easy for me: I didn't work for a newspaper so I had no specific deadline to meet. As soon as they finished and started to filter away, I approached the stars one by one, getting them in as many different poses as I could. The last one I needed was Billy Connolly, who had gone out to get some air. John and I joined him and we were making polite chitchat when he suddenly pointed at the fountain in the middle of Piccadilly. 'Bloody hell! There's a man having a bath!' he chortled.

Sure enough there was a man bathing in the fountain. All his belongings, on the top of which sat a black bowler hat, were folded neatly on the steps. I immediately walked over to the fountain. The man looked at me and laughed. I took two steps back and started taking pictures. I must have taken one whole roll of black and white film before he stood up, walked casually over to his clothes and proceeded to pick them up. He then walked through Piccadilly, completely naked apart from his bowler hat. We were lost for words!

When I got home, I wondered if the pictures of the bather could be worth anything. I locked myself in my darkroom and developed the film. I was pleased with the prints and rang the picture editor of the *Sun* to explain what I had. He told me to bring them along to the office and he would take a look.

Not realizing that that day had been one of the hottest days on record for many a long year, I drove my pictures into Wapping with my heart thudding. The picture editor looked at them and said he would let me know whether or not they would buy them. Not getting an immediate decision, I drove home feeling despondent and none too hopeful. Later that night, however, I got a call from a friend saying that he had bought an early edition of the *Sun* and my pictures were in centre spread with my name in big bold letters underneath. The following Monday, a German newspaper called, wanting to buy the pictures. Not long after that, so did a Swedish paper. I couldn't believe it: I was earning money as a photographer and being paid by national newspapers!

I also got a call from the picture editor of the *Sun*, praising the pictures and thanking me for giving him first refusal. He went on to say that he had heard through the grapevine that I had known the Beatles. After I explained that I had met them several times at Abbey Road Studios, he asked me if I had any pictures that he could buy.

'What sort of pictures are you after?' I queried, praying I had them.

'Do you have any of John Lennon's car?'

Of all the pictures I had of the Beatles, they wanted one of a car!

'As it happens, I do,' I told him. 'I took it as the car was being delivered to the studios on a flat bed truck.'

'Great! Would you bring it in?'

I delivered it that day. It made half a page in the next morning's paper and I had one hundred and fifty pounds in my pocket for one small picture of a car.

Some pictures, like the one of Sir John Gielgud, I never did try to sell, however. Another such picture was one I took of a very gracious lady: Michael Caine's wife, Shakira. She was launching her costume jewellery line and the Press were invited. While chatting with her, I asked if I could take a proper picture of her, and she generously agreed. I later sent her a copy, which she liked and wrote to thank me for. Those pictures – Lord Snowdon is another – simply allowed me to take pleasure in my craft.

Meanwhile, the sale of the flat had gone through. It had taken a year, but we finally had ninety thousand pounds to pay all the debts, put the bankruptcy behind us and put a down payment on a house in Hatch End out of central London. It was a good return on the twenty five thousand we had paid for the flat, but we loved it and were very sad to leave it. The house in Hatch End needed a lot of work, but that wasn't a problem since I knew quite a few people in the building trade and I was a plumber. More importantly, the house had scope to build a darkroom in the garden.

By this time, my career in photography was going so well that I gave up working for Dick, and I didn't see him for a long time. Then one day, I read in the paper that he was building the main gate for Hyde Park. It's still there and it's very beautiful. He also had the only stables in Hyde Park where people could go and ride, so he became very well known. You can never tell how things will turn out!

# 15
# News of the World

I started working freelance for *News of the World* in the late eighties, and then Piers Morgan offered me a full time staff position when he took over as Editor in 1994.

Right at the beginning, I met Trevor Kempster, a clever man who showed me the ropes of investigative journalism. It's not difficult; it just takes balls and sheer determination, which come naturally to me. You don't need to go to college for that. I'm sure there are many things you learn in a college setting, but any good talker who can put him/herself in a variety of unfamiliar situations, assess them and build credibility, can be an investigative journalist. You have to be imaginative and be able to think on your feet, because the situation you're in might be the only chance you're going to get to take the picture you need.

Nobody taught me how to do any of that: it's in-built. I don't consider myself particularly intelligent, but there is an actor in me and I can walk into a room full of total strangers, pretend to be anybody I want, and, by the end of the evening, I will know a *lot* about half a dozen people or more. I can convince people that they have met me before but cannot quite remember where or when. I begin by acting as if I know them and then pick up clues in the conversation, mention places they might have been and just keep on bullshitting. You do have to believe, totally, that you are the person you're pretending to be or it won't work. And it doesn't always work, regardless of how you perform, but that's the chance you take.

It's your demeanour and the way you behave that convinces people. If I go into a restaurant, pretending to be somebody rich and important, I *become* that person. If I haven't booked ahead of time, I convince them that I have, that they must remember me, and that they're under an obligation to find me a table. In those moments, I *am* that person; I believe it, so they believe it. Sometimes it takes over, especially if an investigation takes a while and I've done a substantial run of being some character or other. I believe it to such a degree that I'm still in that mode when I get home, and then Jeannette brings me back down to earth!

Working for a Sunday newspaper meant that I worked on Saturdays and had Mondays off. Tuesday was the first day of the week and nobody did much on that day because all we thought about was drinking. We would come in, do our expenses and then go round to the pub. We were all heavy drinkers and when we came back to the office afterwards, work was out of the question: on more than one occasion, I put my head down and slept beside the typewriter, as did the others.

One guy, Gerry, was a real character we sometimes had to drag out of the pub and just put into a cab. I didn't work with him a lot but his fondness for drink worked well in one story we did

181

on Carmen Proetta in 1992. She was an independent witness in the case following *Operation Flavious*, in which the SAS had shot and killed three IRA members suspected of a bomb plot in Gibraltar. Proetta said the IRA members had been shot after they fell to the ground. As a result, certain British newspapers attacked her character, and she later won substantial damages from them. Gerry and I were sent to check out whether she was as innocent as she claimed. Gerry went a month before me, posing as a Scottish drunkard, which was a good cover and suited him down to the ground. He dressed in dirty old clothes, slurred his speech and, to make it even more convincing, he once hit his head against a wall and let the blood dry down the side of his face. He found out that she had some shady dealings to do with passports and approached her on the pretext of doing a deal.

When I got there, we had to hire a van to do the surveillance and get pictures. The only kind we could get was a motor home that had windows all the way round. I had to be out of sight, and, having nothing that covered the windows properly, we bought black bin liners and covered every window with them, bar the windscreen.

Gerry had arranged to meet Proetta outside a restaurant and, just prior to her arrival, two fellows on motorbikes rode up, looked all round the area and then left - her bodyguards. A few minutes later, she rolled up in a sports car and Gerry went off to meet her, carrying a tape recorder, while I stayed in the car park, taking pictures from inside the van.

It was not long before I was sweating profusely. The sun was at its height and I was in a

My grandparents with eleven of their children.
My dad is back row, third from the left.

Minnie Eliza Goom

Mum and Dad, circa 1930.

... and 40 years later.

Albert Road, my home and playground.
The telegraph pole (foreground) was our cricket stump(s).

The day I got my leather jacket.

1970/71, DJ extraordinaire, with Jeannette beside me.

1976, with Jeannette and Laura.

Laura (seated centre) in the bar with friends at Abbey Road Studios.

Life is good!

Me and my pal, Sunny.

My grandchildren, Ben and Grace.

SHAKIRA CAINE 28th Feb 89

Dear Steve,
    The Photograph is
Sensational. You took years
off my face.
    It was really kind of
you — I appreciate very much.
                Kindest Regards
                    Shakira

Shakira Caine

Lord Snowdon

With Aldi and Maria in Vitez.

With Stuart White in Vitez.

This haircut cost me a tenner!

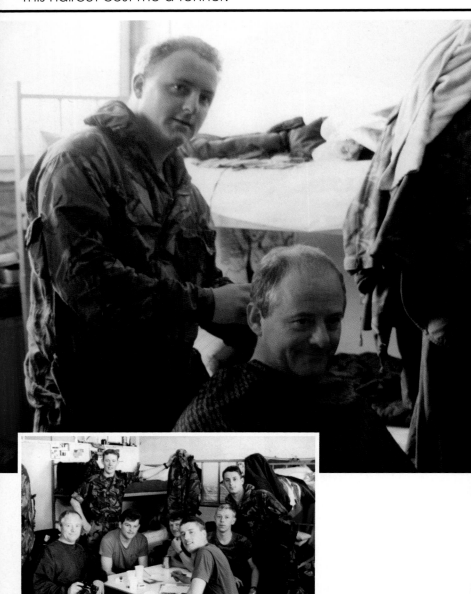

Relaxing at the barracks in Vitez.

Going out with the army.

The Serb who died because I took this picture.

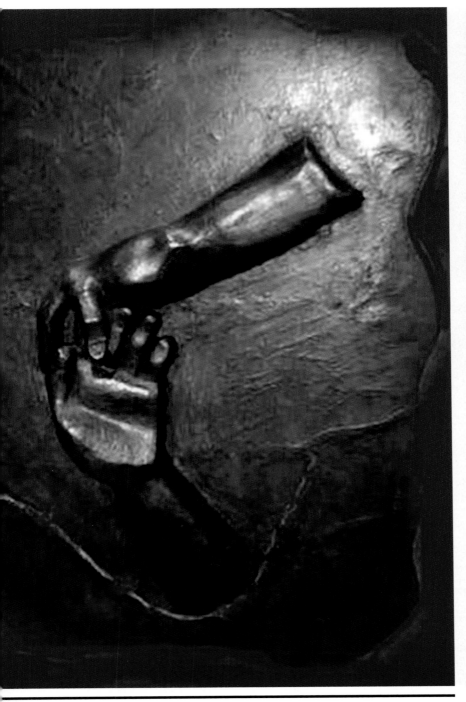

The piece that hangs in the Press area at the NATO offices in Brussels.

Giraffe

Rhino

Hands

Jazz

Blue Horizon

Seaside 3

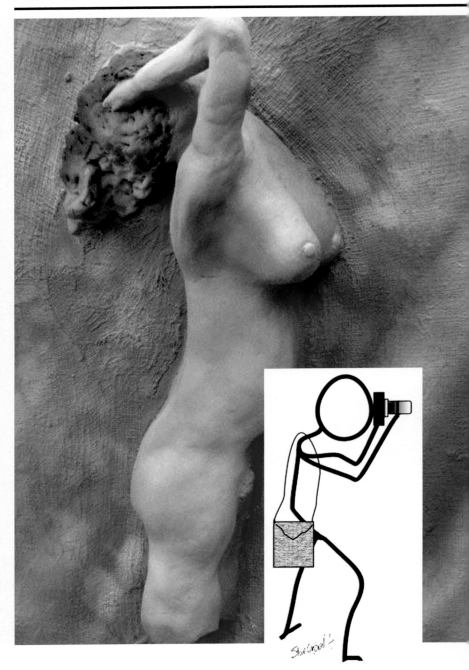

Snapper

plastic 'hot house' of bin liners. I stripped off completely, getting increasingly uncomfortable. I was stark naked, sweat was dripping off me, and then my eyes began to run and feel sore. I carried on taking pictures and tried to ignore the discomfort, but my eyes were getting worse and I was getting dizzy. I thought it was dehydration, although I was drinking lots of water, and by the time the witness left Gerry and went into the restaurant, I was feeling nauseous and ill. Little did I know I was poisoning myself: black plastic bags give off toxic fumes, especially in heat, because of the petroleum content.

I put on my underwear and drove round the corner to wait for Gerry and have a pee. I must have been looking pretty awful because when I got back in the van, the bodyguards came up on their motorbikes and asked if I was all right. It was then that I realised I was not only sitting there in my underwear, but also exposing myself! I felt so ill, I had forgotten to rearrange things! They were really good and helped me out of the van. Gerry, who had done a wide, diversionary birth rather than come straight back to me, came round the corner while they were giving me water and made a sudden mad dash. He thought they were beating me up!

It all turned out well, though. It was a good story, and I got a nice bonus and a bit of an accolade from the Managing Editor Stuart Kuttner, for my pains.

When we gathered evidence of illegal activity, we always turned it over to the police, but they rarely acted on it. Another typical example was a big story in all the papers about a couple whose yacht had been overrun by pirates in the Carribean. The husband had disappeared and the woman was flying back to this country with her child. The story seemed a bit far-fetched and our remit was to find out if she was telling the truth. I was working with another journalist, John Hellings, and we had arranged to meet her at a hotel near Heathrow.

We had a copy of her original statement to the police, and we decided to play 'good cop, bad cop'. I was the bad cop and I must admit I gave her a really hard time, which I did not feel good about because the baby was tired and crying most of the time. According to her, she had been locked in a cabin with the baby, and she could just hear what was going on out on deck through the air vents; she maintained she had heard her husband being killed. I had a plan of the boat, which included the air vents, and I asked her which cabin she had been locked in. From the location of it, I could see she could not possibly have heard anything through the air vent. She was aft, and the murder was supposed to have taken place near the bow end of the boat. She might have heard something if the air vent had been directed out towards the deck, but it wasn't; it vented through into the hallway, deep inside the interior of the boat. I could not understand why the police hadn't picked up on that. She also said that, through the vent, she saw her husband being dragged off the boat. She couldn't have. It was not possible.

For some reason the Caribbean police had not asked the questions I thought were obvious. It was clear to us that she was lying. For what reason we never found out, because she got away with it, but probably to get his life insurance. The police interviewed us and there was a big enquiry, but nothing came of it.

From the start with *News of the World*, I had a good combination for building a reputation for getting the pictures others could not: my experience as a trained investigator, what I had learned from Trevor and my own chutzpah. I began as I meant to continue, using every thing I had.

In June 1989, when Mandy Smith married Bill Wyman, there was a big party at the Dorchester. A magazine had the exclusive and the Press were definitely not invited. However, *News of the World* wanted inside pictures and sent me. There were bouncers everywhere, and the rest of the Press waiting outside, as usual, fingers up their tripods! They were all at the side entrance, which led into the ballroom where the party was, so I went in the main entrance where there were no bouncers, just the room cordoned off and a *Private Function* sign next to a woman checking invitations.

I went downstairs to the basement to look for something I could use to get in. I found a white coat in the boiler room, but that was no good. I carried on looking and eventually found a dirty waistcoat that looked like someone had been polishing with it. I didn't think I would be allowed in because I was wearing brown trousers, which were not formal wear either, but I put the waistcoat on, thinking I had nothing to lose. On the way back, I picked up an ashtray and a bottle of water and just walked right in. The woman at the door looked at me, but to her I was a waiter. Either she didn't notice or didn't comment on the polish all down the side of the waistcoat! As soon as I got in, I went into the toilet and took it off.

I got some strange looks because I wasn't dressed for the occasion, but I was *in*. I chatted to the guests like I was one of them, and I got lots of pictures. The photographer, Terry O'Neill, was there, taking private pictures. Although he went to school with my brother, he didn't recognise me at first, but, seeing a photographer, he came over, talking very posh one minute and then saying to me, 'What the fuck are you doing here?'

'I'm a guest.'

'You fucking ain't! You're a photographer! You're Steve Grayson, aren't you? *News of the World!*'

Despite my protests, he went to the bouncers and had me thrown out. Of course, I went out the door where all the Press boys were and, as soon as they saw me, they knew I'd got the pictures they wanted!

Later that summer, there was nothing going on and Mandy Smith had gone to some health clinic. One lovely sunny Tuesday, I wanted to be out in the sun rather than going into town, so I rang the office and suggested I go and find out about her. The Picture Editor didn't think I'd get anything, plus dozens of photographers would be there, but he told me to have a go.

The health clinic was a large farm and the guy who ran it was making a fortune. You couldn't see them, but in the grounds there were little huts where the guests stayed; the idea was to live the simple life in the sheds and then eat together in something that looked like a big, old army hut.

As usual, the Press were all waiting at the front entrance for Mandy Smith to come out. There was no chance of her walking out; if she came out at all, it would be in a limo, which would not make an interesting shot. I could have got in the back way but I didn't want to; there would be the problem of explaining why I was in there if I got caught, and I would only be able to get a 'snatch' picture – a quick one.

I went home, had a think about it, and then rang the place. I spoke to a woman, said I was a botanical photographer with a magazine (a fictitious one) and asked if I could photograph the fantastic plants we'd heard they had. She put me through to the owner.

'Why would you want to take pictures of plants?' he asked reasonably.

'Well, it's obvious really,' I said, making him feel a bit silly. 'I'm taking the pictures so that we can identify them. We'll say where they're growing, so you get a bit of advertising.'

'Oh, of course!' he said. 'Could you put my name in, as well?'

'Yes, we can do that,' I said.

'What time would you like to come? Only we've got Mandy Smith staying with us and the Press are all here at the front.'

'Mandy who?'

'You know, Mandy Smith, married to a Rolling Stone.'

'Oh, I won't bother then,' I said. 'I don't want to mix with those arseholes. I'm not that sort of photographer.'

'You took the words right out of my mouth,' he said, 'but there's a little side gate. Tell me what time you're coming and I'll let you in.'

I left my car some way away and walked up to the place, found the gate and, sure enough, some guy let me in and took me to the owner's office, which was also a hut. The farm spread over many acres and he directed me away from where the Press were up in trees and everywhere. I was completely by myself, and every time anybody came along, I was here and there taking pictures of plants.

After a couple of days, Mandy Smith came jogging past. I carried on with the plants and didn't take a picture of her because, now I had access to the place, I knew I would get pictures of her eventually. Sometimes you need to go for a quick shot, but this wasn't one of them. A quick picture of Mandy Smith wouldn't have been anything more than the Press outside the gate and up the trees might get. I wanted more: I wanted pictures of the hut she was staying in and I wanted her to take me there. I didn't have any qualms about deceiving her because she had married a star, and those people relish the attention.

A while later, she ran back; I still didn't take a picture. I thought maybe she took the same route everyday, so I was there at the same place, same time the next day. Sure enough, she came jogging along. This time, I picked some flowers and stood up. 'Absolutely gorgeous!' I exclaimed as she ran by.

'Oh yes! They are!' she said, stopping. 'What are you doing?'

'I've got a commission to take pictures for a brochure,' I said.

'It's a beautiful place,' she said.

'Yes, it is. My name's Steve, by the way.'

'I'm Mandy.'

'Pleased to meet you, Mandy. You look fabulous.'

'Thank you. I've been doing some working out.'

'Well, you do look really fabulous. Let me take a picture of you.'

'Oh no, I don't want my picture taken. Those bastards outside are trying to get pictures of me all the time.'

'Why?' I asked.

'I'm married to one of the Rolling Stones.'

'I'm ever so sorry! I didn't recognise you. I still don't. I just thought you and the flowers would make a lovely picture. It's only for me.'

'Oh, okay,' she said.

And I took her picture, just like that, in her running gear.

'See you tomorrow,' she said, after I thanked her. And off she jogged.

I made sure I was there the next day when she came along.

'Hi Steve, how are you?' she called, and came to a stop beside me.

'I asked somebody about you and they said you're married to Bill Wyman,' I said. 'Congratulations! I'm sorry I didn't recognise you.'

She just shrugged and smiled.

'You must have a lovely place here,' I said nonchalantly, looking down at the flowers.

'No, it's just a hut,' she told me. 'Come and have a look. See what you think of it.'

Off we went! This was what everybody wanted!

'I can't believe this is all you've got!' I said when we arrived. It was a one bedroom shed, no television or anything.

'Come and see round the other side. Wait 'til you see the toilet,' she said, walking ahead of me. I took some quick shots and followed. We had a nice little chat, I got pictures of her inside the place, and then I left. *News of the World* made a spread of it.

That cover came in useful again, around the same time, when the paper got a tip off that somebody living on a farm next to a safari park had shot a tiger. I couldn't get pictures from the gate, so I drove up to the farmhouse. The guy there asked what I wanted and, again, I named a fictitious magazine – an agricultural one, this time - and said I had come to take pictures of farms in the area. I half expected him to tell me to 'piss off', but he didn't. Instead, he gave me a tour of the farm, talking about applying for grants and so on, and watching me take pictures.

It was a classic example of turning someone over. He liked me, thought I was on his side, and invited me into the house. While we had tea and cakes, I casually brought the conversation round to the safari park. He said it was a lovely place but the animals roamed too close to his farm, which he didn't like. That was all he said before changing the subject. I didn't push it, or show any particular interest, so as not to alert him. In fact, we got off the subject altogether. A bit later, though, we got onto the subject of guns, and he took me into the boot room, held up a great big shotgun and said, 'How about this Purdy!' I acted as if I was full of admiration and asked if I could take a picture. He said I could. I then had a picture of him with a great big gun for a story about shooting animals!

He got a phone call while I was there, and told me to make myself at home while he went and took delivery of something. I wandered around and went into a shed where there were two walk-in freezers, which I opened, thinking it strange that he would have them and wondering what he kept in them. I was rewarded with the horrible sight of parts of a donkey hanging there and ... a tiger! I got the pictures, shut the door, waited for him to come back and then left.

I could talk my way into and out of most situations, and I had a little white van that was all rigged out with surveillance equipment and costumes, such as uniforms and overalls, a vicar's shirt front and collar – all kinds of different stuff - which I got from a famous costume place in Camden Town. One of the marvellous things about it was that it was like being a chameleon: you could go into the van and come out as somebody else.

I was on another job when the paper rang me, one time, and asked me to go with my van and get pictures of an Irish woman who was allegedly being paid one thousand pounds a time to marry a succession of men for convenience, enabling them to stay in this country. One of the staff photographers had been sitting outside her house for days and hadn't managed to get any pictures; it looked like she had guessed, or been tipped off, that somebody was onto her.

When I got there, the other photographer was still there and said he hadn't seen her. I looked up at the house, wondering what to do because the other job I was on was an important one and I needed to get this done quickly so that I could get back to it. Her house was a low-income housing association type of place, and I noticed that the glass was broken in one of the windows. That gave me an idea. I went back into the van, put on some overalls, got the little tool bag I had and went knocking on the door. We were hoping the woman would open it, and then the photographer could get the picture. That was all we wanted; the newspaper already had the evidence against her. I kept on knocking and, eventually, a really rough Irish fellow came to an upstairs window and asked me what I wanted. I told him I was from the housing association and I'd come to mend the window. He went back in for a minute and then came back.

'Fuck off!' he said.

'Sorry?' I said.

'Me mam says 'fuck off'.'

'Excuse me!' I said. 'I'm not leaving until your mother comes out.'

Another fellow appeared beside him, lending him support. 'You 'eard my brother! Fuck off!' he said.

'Look, I've come to do a load of work in here,' I said. 'Why are you telling me to go?'

The mother came to the window then, but she was behind the two fellows and not clearly visible enough to get a picture. She must have told them to let me in because one of them came down and opened the door. I went in, wondering how on earth I was going to get this picture. It was the most disgusting, revolting place: there were clothes piled up in the corners and there was a horrible, musty, mildewy smell of damp clothes mixed with the sour smell of stale cigarette smoke.

'Where's your mother?' I asked, as I followed this big lout up the stairs and into a filthy, smelly bedroom.

'She won't see you,' he said. 'She's gone back to bed.'

It was the middle of the day, but somehow I wasn't surprised.

'Here's the window. Fix it!' he added aggressively.

The other brother wandered in as I went to the window and rummaged in my tool bag, all the time rattling my brain. 'Oh no!' I said. 'I've forgotten my tape measure. I tell you what, I'll get all the other stuff sorted out and worry about the pane of glass afterwards.'

'What other stuff?'

'Didn't you get the letter?' I asked, looking surprised. 'There's a lot of work scheduled. We're replacing the lino with carpet - it won't be best quality, but it'll be better than lino – and we're building wardrobes for you.'

'Oh, me mam needs wardrobes,' one of them said.

'Why don't you go and tell her,' I suggested, hoping that would entice her to come out. 'I'm sure she'd like to know all about it if she didn't get the letter.'

One of the brothers went in to her and came out alone. 'Thank you very much,' he said.

'Is your mother coming out? I'd really like to explain all this to her.'

He just shook his head.

Now, all I could do was stall for time. 'I really need a tape measure. I must have left mine at my last job,' I explained. 'Have you got one I could borrow?'

'No, mate,' said one, as two heads shook in unison and four eyes stared at me, waiting for my next move.

'Here's what we'll do then,' I suggested. 'You're about five foot ten, and you're about six foot one; if you both lie end to end on the floor, I'll know how long the room is.'

They thought that was a fantastic idea and both arranged themselves on the floor. I got my camera out and took a picture. Although I didn't need one, it was a way of having my camera ready if the mother came out. They jumped up, looking like they were going to annihilate me. 'What are you taking pictures for?' one of them bellowed, as I backed away.

'You people are really difficult,' I complained. 'The reason I'm taking a picture is so that, when I get back, I can work out how long the room is.'

'Oh, of course! Sorry mate,' one of them said, 'Come on Seamus!' And they both got down and did the width for me as well. So, I took another picture I didn't need.

'What about the wardrobes?' one of them said.

'Stand by the wall with your arms out,' I said. So he did, and I took more pictures. 'Now, we have to get into that room,' I said, pointing to the room the mother was in.

'Oh, no, you can't go in there. That's me ma's room.'

'How am I going to measure for the cupboards and carpets then?'

He saw the sense of that and went in to ask her, nodding her consent as he came out. Minutes later, she appeared - a vision wearing a long, dirty, old-fashioned nightdress, and broken spectacles, taped up and hanging on a piece of string round her neck. She looked bloody awful! No one would have married her for real, and here I was, having to make up to her, calling her a lovely lady and telling her I needed to talk to her about the wardrobes and so on.

'Just get on with it. I need to get back to bed,' she said.

I went into her room and it really stunk; there were more piles of clothes in the corners and full ashtrays, newspapers, pizza boxes - all kinds of rubbish – on the floor around the bed. One of her sons came in and stood against the wall with his arms out.

'What are you doing, you silly sod?' she asked.

'We're measuring for wardrobes, Ma.'

'That's a good idea,' she said.

I still hadn't got a picture of her, but I took another picture of her son.

'Can you do me a favour and put a little cupboard over there?' she said, pointing across the room. 'I've no storage space at all.'

'Come over!' I said, as her son was about to jump over and 'measure'. I grabbed hold of her arm and practically frog-marched her over to the wall. 'Put your arms out!' I said. She did. Finally, I got the picture!

We found out afterwards that her sons worked for the IRA. Again, we gave all the information to the authorities, but nothing came of it.

# 16
# Adventures with Roger

Roger Insall was a features editor with whom I did a lot of investigations. He was extremely good at his job and *had* to get the story; if it wasn't working out, he'd lose his temper. He was also one of the funniest men you could ever go out with and we had a lot of laughs.

We were in Beverly Hills around the time when the film *Cocktail* came out and we went into a bar where the staff were all throwing bottles up in the air and round their backs. I could not resist ordering two *Black and Deckers*. The barman stopped slinging bottles around and said, very politely, that he'd never heard of them and could we tell him how to make them. Roger told him they were two parts W-D40, one part graphite, one part white spirit and a touch of orange juice. The barman still didn't get it and just apologised for not having the necessary ingredients. Americans! They're polite, but they're very thick sometimes!

Also a bit strange, like the time we were staying at the Beverly Hilton and we wanted to go to Rodeo Drive one day. It's only about a mile away and it was a lovely day, so we decided to walk. We had just crossed the road when a police car pulled up beside us and the driver asked us what we were doing. We explained we were just walking to Rodeo Drive. 'Do not walk, Sir,' this police officer said. 'Get a cab.' We explained that we were English and used to walking. 'Please get a cab, Sir. Anyone walking looks suspicious.'

Needless to say, when he'd gone, we carried on walking.

Years ago, *News of the World* did not have much investigative equipment. I had one of the first video cameras but they were big and heavy, and there was no possibility of hiding one on your person. I came up with the idea of camouflaging it; using watercolour (so that I could remove it later), I painted flowers or greenery all over it and hid it in pot plants. There I would be in some hotel, recording with a Nagra strapped to my back and the camera hidden in a plant. *News of the World* thought it was a brilliant idea.

You couldn't do it everywhere, of course. Roger and I went to Bangkok in 1992 and I had to come up with another of these make-do-and-mend ideas. A Thai national in the British Embassy was illegally issuing visas, giving them to the police chief, who would then sell them to people who wanted to get into Britain. We were sent to try and catch them at it. Roger went on all the Thailand stories because his wife was Thai and he spoke the language to some degree.

Through our contact informant, we got the story and we wanted to get pictures of the guy inside the embassy. We went to check it out and it was obvious we could not walk in with a big camera sporting a big silver lens. I bought a rucksack and cut a hole to fit the camera, arranging it all in such a way that light would not reflect off the lens. Everything was manual then, so we switched it on, in we went, and we got footage of him working. We then needed proof that he was taking money.

We were staying in a beautiful hotel, eating lunch beside a swimming pool, when we had the informant ring him up and ask if he could help get his family into England. He said he could, so we all went to the embassy and entered separately. I had to be somewhere I could set up recording equipment as well as the camera, so I got in amongst the leaves of a huge rubber plant. I was relying on the fact that, if nobody was looking for a guy with a camera, I wouldn't be noticed. So there I was, filming with a zoom lens, a large microphone and recorder on the floor in front of me. The informant gave the forms to the corrupt Thai official and we recorded him telling the informant that he would make sure the application was processed, and that the informant had to collect the visa from the police chief and pay him. Suddenly, I was tapped on the shoulder and heard a Thai voice, presumably asking what I was doing there. I turned to see a policeman glaring at me. I didn't react with guilt or fear, as he probably expected; I shushed him and beckoned for him to come closer and have a look. And he did! That gave me enough time to get the footage I needed, and then I just gave him a fistful of barts (Thai currency) and left.

Next, we needed filmed evidence against the police chief. It was arranged that the informant would meet him at the American Hotel. We rigged up a camera in a plant pot and were ready at the appointed time to film our man and the police chief completing the transaction of a visa in exchange for money.

For some reason, the police chief became suspicious of us. We didn't realise this, at first, and later agreed to meet him, at his request, in a certain room in the same hotel. When we got to the room and a young Thai girl came in, Roger immediately recognised that we were being set up. 'This girl is going to strip off any minute, shout 'Rape!' and we've had it,' he said. All of a sudden, there was a knock on the door and two big guys came in carrying a very small television, which didn't need two guys to carry it. Obviously, they were undercover police. Roger immediately said, 'I think we'll get out of here.' And we ran like hell! They chased us, but we got down the stairs, out of the hotel and into a taxi, forgetting that there's so much traffic in Bangkok nothing ever moves. The cab just stood there; we looked at each other, paid the guy and ran like hell again.

Everybody is on the make in Thailand and, inevitably, they found out where we were staying. We came back to our hotel, one evening, and there were two soldiers sitting in the foyer with the police chief. I spotted them and before I even had time to tell Roger, they had come over to us. They were pretending to be friendly, and the police chief asked us to go with them to their car because he wanted to talk to us. We got in the back of the car with one of the soldiers; the other got in the front to drive, and the police chief was in the passenger seat. As we drove off, he pulled a gun, turned and pointed it at Roger's head. Instinctively, I took a picture! Naturally, Roger was rigid with fear and mad as hell.

I could have got him killed. For some reason I cannot explain, however, I did not believe that killing was in the police chief's mind, and it was my job to get a picture.

They took us to a back room in another hotel to question us. They wanted to know who we were, whom we worked for and so on. We had to say something and, in the end, we said we were British Secret Service. While Roger turned every shade of purple and then green, I said, 'Go ahead and kill us, but the Secret Service know we're here and know we're with you, so you'll be next.'

Since I'm here to tell the tale, they obviously let us go. And, eventually, the police chief was charged … but let off!

While we were there, we went to the notorious Thai prison, the 'Bangkok Hilton'. There was an English guy in there, sentenced to five years for stealing a Thai passport, and *News of the World* wanted us to get an interview with him.

We didn't have a visitor's order, but we didn't need one. We got to the gates, which are very imposing, and paid the guards: first the one at the gates, then two more who were sitting, drinking and smoking, further inside the prison and asked whom we wanted to see. One of them took us to where he was, and, as we went along, there were people putting their arms through the bars, wanting food and cigarettes. It was *diabolical* and the smell was indescribable: urine and excrement mixed with body odour, and all the prisoners were stripped to the waist because it was so hot.

The English guy was in a large cell of wall-to-wall people, mostly Thai. There was one toilet between three cells, permanently blocked, and nobody cared. There were no washing facilities apart from one tap near the blocked toilet, where they lined up in the morning just to rinse themselves down. He'd been there seven months and though he'd done wrong, he didn't deserve that. Poor bastard had tried to steal an English passport and got a Thai one by mistake, or so he said. We gave him cigarettes and he wanted food but we didn't have any. He said that if we gave money to the guards they would get him some, so we did that. We also had to pay to get out. It was a terrible place. I felt really sad for the guy and wondered, *what kind of a world are we living in?*

The story never made it into the paper because it wasn't interesting enough for the *News of the World*: no sex or drugs; no vicars involved.

Roger obviously knew his way around and he played a few tricks on me. After we had been to the prison, we went to a very famous district in Bangkok called Soa Cowboy, where all the sex clubs are. We were in one of these places and Roger told me that when I wanted a drink I should ring a bell that was there. I thought nothing of it and duly rang it. All at once, girls came from everywhere, some half naked, all wanting me to buy them a drink – the bell meant you were buying a round!

There were also very pretty dancing girls and you could pay a few barts to dance with one of them. We both had a dance and the one I was dancing with said she sold flowers. She spoke very good English and I talked to her and bought her drinks for a while, and then asked her if she'd like to come back to my hotel. She said she would, but told me she didn't 'do anything' the first night. I told her that was not what I wanted, and we went back to the hotel with Roger and another girl, who kept giggling all the time. Just before we went up to our rooms, the girls said something to each other, in Thai, that looked like a bit of an argument. Roger could speak Thai and it transpired that the 'girl' I was with was a boy, which Roger already knew! He/she was so unbelievably pretty, I never guessed. These 'lady-boys', as they're called, are also called 'butterflies' because they flit from one person to the next.

The next night, when we went back to Sao Cowboy, a girl came up to me, selling flowers. I thought she was another lady-boy and Roger playing tricks again, so I said I didn't want any. She kept on and on, wheedling and pleading, so I grabbed the flowers and smashed them on the side of the bar. This caused a huge commotion! I didn't know, but doing that to flowers is a big insult in Thailand – especially those from a flower girl. They were all ready to pounce on me, so, once again, we had to get out of somewhere very fast!

A few weeks later, we were on a dangerous story in Hong Kong, having a major argument. Roger was not always easy to get along with and I can't even remember what the argument was about, except that he was insisting that I do something that was really stupid and I was refusing. I was driving, at the time, and I got so annoyed that I veered slightly over to the wrong side of the road and pushed hard on the accelerator. I scared the daylights out of him; he was screaming and yelling at me, but whatever he had been insisting that I do was never mentioned again. You had to do things like that with him; if you were meek and mild, he would walk all over you.

Hong Kong was still British then, and it was the first time I had ever seen or paid in a restaurant with the credit card gadget that's brought to the table. Considering the story we were covering, it's an odd detail to remember. We had been given information about drugs being brought from China, via Hong Kong, to the UK, and we were there posing as drug dealers. We were staying at a beautiful hotel in Nathan Road, Hong Kong, sitting in the bar, waiting to meet the guy who was our contact, when a girl turned up instead, saying the fellow couldn't make it. She spoke English well, although she had a twisted scar on her lower lip, which made it difficult for her to talk. She was willing to sell us information about where the drugs were coming from on the Chinese side and how they were smuggled into London, which was what we wanted, so we weren't concerned about meeting the guy.

We all went out for dinner to a famous club she suggested. It was very modern and high-tech: there were chandeliers and beautiful, circular booths, each of which was equipped with a keypad; everything on the menu was numbered and you keyed in the number of what you wanted, and then a lovely waitress would appear with it. It was all very expensive, but we were supposed to be drug dealers, for whom money was no object. So we had a wonderful meal, and she agreed to arrange for us to meet two fellows to discuss how much heroin and cocaine they could get.

She left ahead of us and, as she did, she told us not to forget to ask about the 'special keypad'. I duly called the waitress over and asked. She went away and came back with a different 'menu' covered in pictures of girls, each with a number and a list of services she would provide; there was every 'service' you could imagine, and more besides. We thought this was a story in itself and picked a couple, who appeared very quickly and were very talkative. It was silly really, and we knew it, because *News of the World* wouldn't be interested unless there was a UK connection. Anyway, par for the course, the girls wanted drinks and very dextrously keyed in the numbers of the most expensive ones, which was no less than we expected. We took a few pictures, chatted for a while and had a real laugh because Roger was a lunatic and a very funny man. The girls told us there were rooms at the back of the club where they could take us, but we were only having a bit of fun and didn't take them up on that.

It was when we asked for the bill that the waitress brought this credit card gismo that we thought amazing. The bill came as a surprise too: every number keyed into the keypad, and what it stood for, came up on the bill, including the girls – two hundred and fifty Hong Kong dollars each!

There were lots of meetings in between to establish our credibility, but, eventually, we met two of the drug dealers, both of them Chinese. One of them chain smoked non-stop, and his front teeth were so black I couldn't help thinking that with all the money he had he might at least get his teeth seen to. We had bought a small sample of good cocaine in Hong Kong and showed it to them to indicate the quality we wanted. 'Black Teeth' tested it for purity and showed us a sample of what he had available, which was also good quality, and told us that he could supply us with six kilos but that the drugs were in China, and the deal would have to be done there. We agreed and made the arrangements, but after we left them Roger said he was a bit suspicious of the guy with the black teeth. We rang London to try and find out where the original contact person was, so that we could speak to him, but they didn't know.

That evening, we went to the Press Club for dinner and to meet with an English copper who was out there. We filled him in on everything that was going on and he said there was no way we would succeed in catching them, but we were not interested in hearing that. He also advised us not to go into China because, once we were over there, the Hong Kong police could not help us.

We went ahead with the arrangements, anyway: we got day visas, rented a car and crossed the border to meet two guys we were told would be in a blue Ford Cortina. When we got there, the Cortina was there, but no guys. Roger became even more suspicious because it was a beat up old car and did not look the kind of vehicle drug dealers would be using. Nevertheless, we waited, wondering if they were planning to rob us, although they would have been disappointed. We didn't have any substantial money on us because we were planning to tell them that we would only do the deal in Hong Kong. That way, we could have them nicked and get a great story about intercepting all this cocaine on its way to Britain. We just wanted some pictures at the border – which I planned to take with a hidden camera – and something on tape, to show the route the drugs came.

An hour passed and Roger had to get out for a pee. As he got back in the car, we were suddenly surrounded by a lot more than two Chinese guys, which was a bit worrying, to say the least. 'Relax!' I said to Roger. 'We've got nothing for them to pinch.' We got out and asked if they had the drugs. They said they did, but we could not see them until we showed them the money. I was wearing a safari jacket and I patted all the pockets, showing them and telling them that we did not have the money with us because we would only do the deal in Hong Kong. It was a standoff and we couldn't reach any agreement. Eventually, we just went back to the hotel.

We had meetings with the guy with the teeth again, but he would never agree to bring the drugs to us in Hong Kong; he insisted that it had to take place over the border in China. In the end, nothing happened. We got a good story because we got pictures of this guy, showing us the small packet of cocaine and so on, but it wasn't the massive story it could have been.

I met a triad member five or six years ago, when a policeman, whose wife was Chinese, introduced me to some people at a restaurant. We got chatting and I found out that our original contact had disappeared – probably murdered - and was never seen again. The girl with the scarred lip was actually an informant for both sides – a double agent, so to speak – and was trying to find out if we really were the drug dealers we said we were. And we were right about being set up: they had planned to rob us.

The year following Hong Kong, we were doing a piece in Romania, which was a real shit hole then - unbelievably poor. The destitution had given rise to a lot of crime and the roads were infested with bandits, who would hold foreigners up and shoot them if they refused to give up their money. Luckily, we didn't meet any.

People were going over there, buying girls and then putting them to work as prostitutes in London. To find out if this was true, we went there pretending to choose a couple of girls for prospective buyers. Roger went over first to meet the contact; I was on a story and followed when I'd finished it.

I arrived at this huge communist hotel that had a gigantic hammer and sickle on it. It must have been beautiful when it was new, but it was now desolate and miserable. I was shown to an enormous room, but the bed had a straw mattress, which I could see immediately because the dirty straw was coming out. I caused a fuss and refused the room, not knowing that that was all they had, until they gave me an even bigger room, still with a straw mattress. I could not help wondering how many years it had been there, and it made me itchy just looking at it. I later took the blankets off and slept on the floor.

I went down to meet Roger for dinner in the dining room. On my way down, I took a wrong turn and found myself up in the gallery above the dining room, which was the size of the Albert Hall, complete with this gallery stretching all the way round it, all wood and very gothic; it must have been magnificent once. The only people in the room below were Roger, sitting with our contact and the two girls he'd arranged for us, a couple dancing and a violinist. Roger saw me and beckoned me down, laughing. Having been there for a couple of days, he knew what was coming.

'You're not going to believe this,' he said, calling the waitress over. She came with the menu, which was the thickness of the bible.

'I can't possibly look through all this,' I fussed.

'They show it to everyone, but they only have one thing: potato and cabbage soup,' Roger informed me, grinning.

'I'll have potato and cabbage soup, please,' I told the waitress dryly. When it came it was greasy but nice, so I was quite happy and asked Roger about a main course.

'There isn't one. This place is too poor for that. But you can have dessert,' said Roger.

'One or two peaches?' the waitress asked when I called her over. I was starving and, assuming they were fresh peaches, asked for two.

Roger started laughing again but would not tell me why. Seconds later, I saw the waitress pushing a dessert cabinet towards us, filled with car parts!

'Is this a joke?!' I said.

'This is for your pleasure to look,' the waitress told me solemnly and sweetly.

'Where are my peaches?'

'I bring them soon.'

So there we were, looking at Zenith engine parts. All the shops in the reception area were closed because they had nothing to sell, and there was no one with money to buy anything. Display cases usually full of jewellery or gifts were all full of Zenith car parts. They were all they had.

Finally, my peaches arrived … two tins of them, opened!

In the absence of food and every other comfort, there was plenty of vodka and Sambuca, so we got drunk a lot to kill the hunger pangs.

As we were in Transylvania, we decided to use the Dracula hook in the story. The castle was on a hill and we drove up there with the girls one evening. We found a cemetery and it seemed the perfect place to take pictures, especially since it was getting dark. I got them to pose around the gravestones, looking horrified and scared, and I knew I'd got some good shots.

When we got back to the hotel, the contact was angry that we'd done this and wanted us to take more serious pictures of the girls. It didn't matter to us so to keep him happy we agreed, and they went off to get ready. Getting ready, it turned out, was getting undressed; they thought the prospective buyer would want to see everything so they came back stark naked, except for high heels, which just made me and Roger laugh. I did take the pictures to appease the contact, but for the paper we used the ones we took in the graveyard. The story was something about bringing Dracula's girls to London.

Our contact had to drive us to the airport at night to get our flight back, and it was very foggy. He was really worried about the bandits on a particularly dangerous road we had to use, but, obviously, we made it back to tell the tale.

# 17
# The Randy and the Wayward

*News of the World* paid my salary for nearly ten years and I did not care what kind of story I was on, as long as I was earning money. Nevertheless, I genuinely had a conscience about everything I did. There are things I'm terribly ashamed of, and I've had sleepless nights after some stories, thinking about the person we had turned over for no other reason than some cheap sensationalism that would be used for chip paper an hour later.

One such story, which ended tragically, ran in June 1992. A journalist I frequently worked with was Mazher Mahmood and we were asked to get a story about wife swapping in the south of France. An English chef and his girlfriend were advertising 'sexy fun mini breaks' at their chateau. This included a big dinner party with as much champagne - or anything else - as you could drink and as much food as you could eat, before all piling into each other (for want of a better way of saying it!). We duly booked ourselves and partners in for a weekend. We didn't want any other couples to come, though. With Mazher, me and partners pretending to swap it was safe; any more people would have complicated things. So Mazher found out who else was booked in for that weekend, rang them and put them off. I was not involved with that aspect, so I don't know how he did it, but there were ways of finding things out, at that time, which would be illegal now.

Mazher was posing as a doctor and taking his girlfriend. It was best to just say I was a photographer, and then I wouldn't have to hide my cameras and could get pictures more easily. That took care of my cover, but I needed a partner and I couldn't find anybody to go with me. In the end, I asked my wife. I knew, of course, that she wouldn't go if she knew what it was all about, so I neglected to tell her!

We flew to France and drove down to the town nearest to the chateau, at which point we had to split up. We had booked as separate couples who didn't know each other, so we could not arrive together. Jeannette and I went first and left Mazher and his girlfriend to arrive a little later than us. At this point, I had to tell Jeannette why we were really there. She was not altogether surprised, but she was very upset. I was apologising and pleading with her to pretend to swap with Mazher's girlfriend, explaining that that was how we would keep the chef and his girlfriend away from us. When she calmed down, she was exceptionally good about it and agreed to go along with the pretence.

We took a taxi to what we thought was the chateau. It stood in beautiful countryside in the middle of nowhere and was deserted - nobody was in. We had no option but to hang around waiting. Before long, a fellow happened to come walking along the road and I asked if he knew where the people from the chateau were. 'Ah! Ze wife swapping!' he said. I'll never know if it was an open secret or he knew from experience because he told me we were at the wrong place, and I was more concerned about how far away the right one was; I had let the taxi go.

As it turned out, we did not have far to walk, and when we finally got to *the* chateau, the chef and his girlfriend led us into a big room where there was a table filled with every kind of hors d'oeuvre you could imagine. We enjoyed sampling those and had drinks before going to our rooms to change for dinner.

The girlfriend showed us into a stunningly beautiful room when we came down and sat down with us at a massive round table, set for dinner. When Mazher and his girlfriend came in, she introduced us and we sat making conversation, as if we were strangers, and had more drinks before the food was brought out, all of which was absolutely gorgeous, special wines – the lot. The chef did a superb job, and after he'd cooked everything he came and ate with us.

Brandies followed and a few hours passed before we were taken into yet another lovely room. The chef did not immediately join us, and his girlfriend left the double doors of the room open, which we thought nothing of, at the time. A short while later, we realised she'd had a reason: the chef, clearly visible through the open doors, was making an entrance, walking down the stairs completely naked except for a 'posing pouch' – a silk jock strap! None of us dared look at each other, in case we laughed, as he began going backwards and forwards, dancing about, rubbing his 'posing pouch' and trying to get somebody to go over to him. He was as thin as a rake, poor sod, and he just looked stupid.

While he continued to cavort, the girlfriend went upstairs. Heaven knew how she would be dressed or what she would do when she came down! Things were heating up! To keep the chef at bay, Jeannette went and sat on Mazher's knee, and Mazher's girlfriend came to sit on mine.

Within minutes, the chef's girlfriend came downstairs wearing a see-through cat suit and carrying a whip, with which she tapped us all on the behind before she joined the chef. It was quite the spectacle: all of us fully dressed while they were prancing about, practically naked, with nobody to swap with. It all started getting very uncomfortable when they sat on the couch and started performing, obviously thinking we would start too. When we didn't, the chef got up, now minus the posing pouch, came walking round to Jeannette and started putting his hand up her dress. I thought she would smack him but she played her part beautifully. 'No, not yet,' she said shyly, standing up and stepping back so that his hand was left in mid-air.

At the same time, the girlfriend had come over and was trying to feel up Mazher's girlfriend! It was all getting too close for comfort and time for us to get to the safety of our rooms. Mazher stood up beside Jeannette and said they were going upstairs. Still living in hope, the chef suggested they stay downstairs and 'do it'. They said they were too shy and left in a hurry. I needed pictures though, and I was worried that the chef, who was obviously disappointed and pissed off by this time, would get fed up and just go upstairs himself.

'Maybe you'd like to go up and get ready,' I said suggestively to Mazher's girlfriend. 'I'll follow you in a minute.'

'Don't keep me waiting,' she smiled, as she went towards the stairs.

'I'm sorry, you seem upset,' I said, turning to the chef.

'It's a pity no one else is here,' he said, basically meaning we were no good - we weren't performing!

'I'm sorry, but I really fancy that girl,' I said. 'I can't wait to get upstairs to her.'

'Can we watch?' he asked.

'What I'd really like is a picture of you two, as you are,' I said enthusiastically, grabbing my Polaroid Instant. We didn't have digital cameras then, so I always carried a Polaroid because it was handy for knowing if you had got a decent picture, which you never knew with an ordinary camera. 'I'll take that up to her,' I said with a lustful smirk, 'and that will really get her going; then you can come up and have a look.'

'Oh, yeah, yeah,' he said.

I got several pictures of both of them before I went upstairs and told Mazher's girlfriend that the chef would be up in a minute to watch! 'We have to make some excuse,' I said. 'Cry! And I'll think of something.' I could hear the chef and his girlfriend coming up the stairs, and all this girl could manage was a whimper. 'No! Really cry!' I urged, and smacked her across the face! I hit her hard; the pain and shock certainly helped her cry. From the look on her face, she also wanted to kill me! 'Bitch!' I shouted, turning to the chef as he came through the door. 'After all that, she doesn't want to do it!'

He huffed and puffed, saying he couldn't believe the way things were turning out. I kept shrugging and agreeing with him, giving the impression that there was nothing I could do about it, until he and his girlfriend stormed off to Jeannette and Mazher's room to see what was happening there.

They had locked themselves in!

'Come on, let me in,' he called, sounding really pathetic by this time.

'No, we're doing it on our own,' I heard Jeannette say. And then she and Mazher started making these noises that really were not at all convincing!

Eventually, the chef and his girl went to bed and we swapped rooms so that Jeannette was back with me and Mazher was with his girlfriend. By this time, Jeannette had had enough and wanted to leave immediately, especially since I had the pictures I needed. I was in no mood to stay, myself, but the place was so remote, we'd had a lot to drink, and I didn't think we would find our way in the dark. I convinced her to stay until morning, promising that we would leave first thing. It was an easy promise because I knew that, following a big breakfast, there was another session planned for the morning, and the weekend wasn't due to end until the next evening. To get out of it, Mazher and I had already planned that I would ring his phone, and he would pretend to be called away on an emergency.

The next morning, I made sure Mazher and his girlfriend had gone down to breakfast and would be settled in the dining room before I dialled his number. When we got down there, to another table full of all kinds of lovely food, including strawberries and champagne, he was pretending to speak to someone, going over the top, as he always did. 'I'll have to operate right away,' he was saying. 'Could you organise the plane for me?'

When he came off the phone, he told the chef he had to leave immediately because one of his patients was dying. The chef was dumbstruck: nothing was working for him!

'Why are you going?' he asked me a little later, as I was bringing our overnight cases downstairs.

'We're getting a lift to the station,' I said. 'We've had a marvellous time, but it just makes life easier.'

'You can stay!' he said, a little desperately. 'We'll give you a lift to the station later.'

I couldn't think of a reason to refuse, but I left our bags by the door and whispered to Mazher to wait for us down the road. After they'd gone, we had to sit chatting and drinking champagne with the chef and his girlfriend, as if we were totally relaxed. Our opportunity came when the girlfriend went upstairs, presumably to get changed again.

'I could murder a cup of coffee,' I said. 'It's a bit early for all this champagne.'

'I'll get some,' he promptly offered, and got up.

'Go!' I said to Jeannette, as soon as he disappeared round the corner to the kitchen.

We grabbed our bags and got out fast.

Always, when we had done a story like that, we had to ring the people involved, tell them the situation and try to get a reaction from them; it's called 'fronting them up'. Mazher rang the chef, who broke down, crying on the phone, when he heard that this story would be in *News of the World*. He then called the editor, saying if the story went in the paper he would kill himself, the reason being that he was divorced and if this got out he would never be allowed to see his children again. He pleaded with her, but she told him that if she listened to every story like that, nothing would ever be printed. A week or two later, we heard that he'd hanged himself in the chateau.

I was very upset, and, for a long time, I couldn't bring myself to tell Jeannette because I knew how upset she would be, too. It was a terrible thing, and I felt responsible. When I talked to Mazher about it, he said the guy shouldn't have been advertising what he was doing if he didn't want to be found out; after all, that kind of story is what newspapers like *News of the World* go after, and everyone knows it; that's what they're all about and the guy should have been more discreet. Although that was true and gave me an argument for continuing to do my job, it didn't change the way I felt. That man had conducted his activities in the privacy of his own home; he was doing nothing illegal and nobody had to be there unless they wanted to be.

You don't join *News of the World* thinking you're going to be doing local 'cat up a tree' stories, of course. But I couldn't help feeling sorry for those people who might have been on the periphery of a story and got drawn into it when it was not really about them. Sometimes I met really nice people – small people - and I did regret that the story was going to ruin them. I would ask myself, *why are we doing this?* Often, it was simply because there was nothing else going on at the time, and I always felt sorry, but never *too* sorry because looking after my family was always my first priority. Whatever anybody else thinks about it, that was my job at *News of the World*, and it was supported by countless readers.

One man who took the news of his imminent embarrassment with some degree of equanimity, however, was David Mellor. It was 1994, the same year as his affair with Antonia de Sancha. He was having an affair with another woman, who happened to live in the same block of flats as Michael Howard, then Home Secretary. The paper wanted sound and visual evidence to prove the affair, but security was very tight because of the Home Secretary's presence, and shots of David Mellor entering the block were not enough because he could have said he was visiting Michael Howard.

I managed to get inside the building and put a listening device behind a radiator on the fourth floor, where the woman lived. Then I went back to my white van to wait. David Mellor, however, was clever. I would see him entering the block and, a minute or so later, I would hear knocking at the woman's door, but they never spoke to each other when he arrived.

This went on for some time, and then I came up with the idea of sending in a female journalist with video and sound recording equipment hidden in her bag. We stuffed a pillow up her jumper to make her look pregnant, and then, the next time Mellor came, she followed him in. He held the door for her and they entered the lift together; he asked which floor she wanted and she said the fourth. Mellor got out at the third – Michael Howard's floor. The journalist got out at the fourth and had nowhere to go. Expecting Mellor to appear at any moment and not wanting to be caught loitering in the hallway, she started back down the stairs. She passed Mellor on his way up! We had him!

When I fronted him up, he nonchalantly told me to go ahead and print the story because he'd given it to all the newspapers! We led with it, though, and Piers Morgan put his appreciation in a letter to me. I still have all those editors' letters because I got a kick out of them - the bonuses that came with them too.

I had a Filofax full of prostitutes and gays: they were my business contacts. We would go round Soho, buy them a drink or a sandwich, get to know them and ask them to give us a ring if they got any interesting clients. Invariably, they would not want to rat on their own clients, but for a lot of money they would give just a name, and it was up to us to find out the rest and catch the person in the act. I also knew the gay scene very well and we had numerous gay prostitutes informing on people - often gay politicians who had not 'come out' and went with rent boys. All men are ruled by their dicks. All journalists and all women know that. Journalists are glad about it!

One funny story, which was like a real-life farce, involved a prostitute who was informing on a high level banker, whom she was meeting once a week at the Selsden Park Hotel. He liked to ring his wife to ask her permission, and she then liked to listen in on the phone: it was all part of the game. I arranged with Beryl, the prostitute, that I would hide in the wardrobe, and she would give me a signal to let me know when to jump out and take pictures.

I went on the Saturday, as arranged, and while she met him for a drink in the bar, I got into the wardrobe, which happened to have louvered doors that I could see through. Half an hour later, they came in and he went into the bathroom, coming out minutes later wearing all black suspender belt, stockings, knickers and bra. They didn't look quite right with his big hairy chest and moustache; he looked a right idiot. He rang his wife, had a few words and then left the phone off the hook so she could hear. Beryl bent over for him and he was pretending to have sex, doggy fashion, but there was no penetration, he was just saying, 'Come on, doggy! Woof! Woof!' Beryl duly 'woofed', climbed off the bed and went round the room on all fours. He started chasing her, clearly aroused, while Beryl was describing everything so that his wife could picture it.

My cue to come out of the wardrobe was 'he's putting me on the leash'. When Beryl said it, I pushed the door, but it wouldn't open. The latch hook had fallen down when I got in, and it was holding the door shut. He heard the sound and straightened up to come over to the wardrobe just as I smashed open the door, jumped out with the camera and said, 'Hi! It's me!' He actually smiled, because he thought it was part of the game, and stood there in his frilly smalls while I took two clear pictures of him.

'My name is Steve Grayson. I'm here on behalf of *News of the World*,' I said, because it was the policy of the paper in situations like that.

Shock registered on his face for a second, and then, choosing flight over fight, he ran out of the room and down the stairs, dressed – or undressed - as he was. Had he thought for a second, he could have saved himself extra embarrassment by realising that the damage was done. As it was, there was a wedding party coming up as he was going down, he grabbed someone's flowers and carried on down, trying to cover himself. I ran after him and saw him get into his Rolls Royce and drive off in knickers and bra!

In situations like that, the adrenalin is unbelievable because you're somewhere you shouldn't be and you've only got minutes or seconds to do something that means losing the story or getting it.

Then there was the luxury. Very often, when Mazher Mahmood and I were working together, if we weren't at one fancy hotel, we were at another. The Lanesborough Hotel, which used to be St George's Hospital, was opened in 1990, and we were there undercover, doing the usual kind of story on a guy who was attached to the hotel. We had a massive four-bedroom suite and our own butler, who had his own pantry and small bedroom!

Unbeknownst to us, Margaret Thatcher was coming to open it. I was in one of the hotel toilets at one point and this guy came in with curly toed Turkish slippers, an old-fashioned green smoking jacket and red velvet trousers.

'Lovely shoes!' I said sarcastically.

'Ooh, they are, aren't they?' he said, obviously gay. We chatted a bit and he said, 'You must come and meet Mummy.'

I went into a big reception room with him; Margaret Thatcher was there, and 'Mummy' turned out to be one of the Lanesboroughs who owned the hotel, so I was *in* with the special guests! It was a marvellous few days: we would be sitting discussing something, feel like a steak and just ring up the butler. We led that life all the time.

The Savoy was another hotel we frequented. When a prostitute gave us a name and we had to find one of the prostitutes he was going with, we often hired a suite of rooms there. We knew all the prostitutes, so it was a question of finding the right one and getting information from her without her knowing who we were.

Mazher dressed up as a rich Arab; I acted as his secretary and pretended to hire the prostitutes for him. We always had a suite of rooms big enough for the 'Arab' to be in another room, so that, while the prostitute was waiting for him to come in, I could chat to her in my role as his secretary, hopefully getting the name we were after recorded on hidden devices. We also hired a big limousine with a driver we knew, so that he could tape conversations when I went to pick them up and bring them back to the hotel. Seeing the big car and knowing they were going to a suite of rooms at the Savoy, the prostitutes never thought the *News of the World* was behind it, and I might get some information while I was talking to them in the back of the car. We'd have it all on tape.

Early in 1993, we were working on a story about a famous jockey. After seeing a few prostitutes and having the typical problem we always had of making excuses and getting them to leave once we had finished talking to them, I suggested to Mazher that I pose as his wife to get the next one out. We laughed about it because I would have to dress up and be ready to come in, in case a verbal bluff didn't work. I rang the paper, not really expecting any cooperation, but they went along with it and hired a long black abaya, veil, handbag and women's shoes.

When we got the prostitute to the hotel, she was really difficult to talk to: she just wanted to get the job done, get her money and leave. In the end, I just decided to be blunt and get straight to the point. 'You'll get one thousand pounds if you take it up the back,' I said, meaning sodomy. (You get used to saying things like that when dealing with the sex industry.) She said she would, which confirmed on tape that she was a prostitute. I told her she would get five hundred up front and the rest once she had done the job, and I then carried on to get a recorded shopping list of what she would do. It was more than we needed but I wanted to get to the more perverse services; the jockey was into kinky stuff and I was still trying to get his name on tape, if he was a client of hers.

'So, you get all kinds of different requests?' I said conversationally.

'Oh, yeah! I had this strange, short, little fellow a few weeks ago,' she said. 'He said he was a jockey and he was a weird one, but he had plenty of money.'

She went on to tell me a few of the things he liked and, finally, his name. We'd got what we

224

needed and now we had to get her to leave. This was the cue for Mazher, who was listening from the next room, to come in as the Arab. He was very charming, saying how pretty she was, and I told him we had agreed on five hundred pounds to start with. He casually took out a bundle of money – about two thousand, which the paper had sent over by courier – and gave her five hundred as if it was nothing. I then made my excuses, 'reminding' him of some work I had to do, and he talked to her for a few minutes to give me time to go and dress up as his wife. I put all this stuff on: the black dress, the veil, the shoes, and then rang the room, as we'd pre-arranged.

'Yes? What is it?' he said when he answered. He paused for a minute and then said, 'Oh no! Get rid of her! Get rid of her!' He put the phone down and I could hear him telling the prostitute, 'My wife's in the building. You've got to go.'

She wouldn't. She knew Mazher had all that money in his pocket and she demanded the other five hundred pounds. From her point of view, with his wife about to show up, she had a good chance of getting it.

That was my cue. In my own voice I shouted, 'Madam, please! Madam, please!' And then I burst in as the wife, jabbering and pretending to speak Arabic. Mazher is Pakistani and he answered back in his own language. I threw the handbag at him and then sat down with my arms folded. Unbelievably, the prostitute still wouldn't leave. Mazher was saying, 'Get out! You've got to get out!' but she just kept on about the five hundred pounds, and then asked where *I* was! I had to just sit there, without laughing, until, finally, she got fed up and left. I don't know how we both kept straight faces, and we collapsed with laughter right after she left, it was so funny. We only ever did it once though, because it was nerve-wracking and didn't work as efficiently as we thought it would!

We had a lot success under the guises of rich Arab and secretary, however. In 1996 we got a tip off about a couple of former SAS guys starting up a security business and bringing in serving SAS soldiers to work for them on the side, which of course they shouldn't do. Mazher was posing as a rich Arabic sheikh, visiting the country and needing to be looked after. As usual, I was his personal assistant. We booked a suite at the Royal Garden Hotel, this time, because it was just re-opening after a major renovation and we thought it would add kudos to the story.

The SAS guys were quite cautious when I rang: they told me that they only took certain clients and asked me to go to their office.

It was situated in Bond Street, above an art dealer's, and it was very new; it was like going into an intelligence agency that had been recently set up. They were obviously military men and kept me waiting in an outer room, which is an old military tactic to see if I would start sweating or showing signs of nervousness that might indicate I was hiding something - like my true identity! I knew this, and even though I was nervous on the inside, I didn't show it.

When I got in, they started interviewing me about the 'Arab sheikh'. I made up what I could but explained that I couldn't tell them too much because of confidentiality and his insistence on anonymity while he was here. When they asked me questions I couldn't answer I also turned the interrogation round and asked what proof they had that they were ex-SAS. I wanted them to say they had serving SAS soldiers working for them, so I put them down a bit by suggesting that they were just like ex-coppers going into detective work. Put a dent in the ego at the right moment, and you often get what you want to hear, which is what happened.

They charged an exorbitant fee – about five hundred pounds per day for each officer – and they thought we would need about five. I agreed to that, plus expenses, and then left to wait for their decision. Needless to say, with that much money on offer, they soon rang me and took the job.

Two of them came up to the suite the day before the 'sheikh' was due to fly in and asked if they could make one of the bedrooms into a 'command room'. They then went all over the hotel, checking lifts and stairwells, and made a plan of the floor we were on, with instructions about who was covering what area. It was all very militaristic and added interesting details to the story. They wanted to meet the 'sheikh' at the airport, which would have been awkward, so I told them that would not be necessary because he had that all arranged. What they did not know was that we wanted to get pictures of them covering the entrance to the hotel, standing there with the security company logo on their jackets and meeting him on arrival.

An unforeseen bonus was that one of them knew the hotel manager, so, when he explained that they had a VIP arriving and would be taking over the reception area, the manager accepted it because he knew the SAS connection. We could not have planned it better!

The 'sheikh' duly arrived. The security guys opened the limousine door for him, surrounded him and were actually holding people back to let him through. This was the power of money. We had no personal power, but with money we could employ serving SAS, practically commandeer a hotel and have everyone assuming that one fellow, in dress-up, was foreign royalty.

I was parked across the road in my white van, taking pictures of everything.

The SAS involvement was a good story in itself, but the paper always wanted the usual drugs and prostitutes involved, so we had to try for that too. When I went into the 'command room' to give them the details of where we were going that night, all of which they intended to check out, I also told them I was really worried because the 'sheikh' wanted prostitutes and you could not be sure who you were getting. 'Leave it to us,' they said. I got the girls in and the security guys questioned them about health and so on before allowing them in to visit the 'sheikh'.

We all went out for dinner at another big hotel and every time the waiter brought a dish to the 'sheikh' the security guys intercepted him, took the dish and brought it to our table. Everyone was looking, but nobody said anything because they didn't know who we were and we appeared to be important. The next night we all went to a club, where we were taken to a VIP room and drugs were brought to us on request. We later turned the place over for that reason.

It all cost a fortune, but I got fabulous pictures and the story made the centre pages.

The adrenalin rush of a story like that is *incredible*. You're hyped, but then it's a real 'downer' when you go home and life is normal. Jeannette knew when I'd done a good story and it had been successful because I would be miserable for a couple of days. I found everyday life boring and I couldn't talk about a lot of the stuff I did, either. I remember a dinner party we had: some friends of ours had brought a couple round – a teacher and her husband, who was a minor politician - and I was in a typically awful mood following a good story. I said a couple of things and this teacher started saying I was funny, which annoyed me because I wasn't intending to be funny. Then she said I reminded her of Les Dawson and I saw red. I was very rude, saying she reminded me of a bucket of shit, and everything went quiet. The husband said something about never having heard anybody say such a thing, and I told him he should get out more. Needless to say, they left and we haven't seen them since.

They were really bad moods because I had been on such a 'high' and it was like coming down off a drug. There was the excitement of investigations, pretending to be someone I wasn't - often for days at a time - and the possibility of being found out. I was living in multiple worlds, and the real one paled by comparison. If it was the high life in some hotel suite, I could order whatever I wanted, never worrying about the money because we just had to ring the paper, and they'd send it round by courier. Then I'd go home and be expecting Jeannette to wait on me. She would just say, 'Sorry! Go back to the Savoy!' She would not stand for any nonsense, and she has kept my feet firmly on the ground. She has never allowed me to forget exactly who I am!

It could go to your head if you fell into the trap of believing the fantasy. For me, it was always just a job – a good job, living the high life so often, but a job nonetheless. I always wanted to go home afterwards because I was not in awe of that life. In fact, if I was away for a while on a yacht or in some sun-soaked place, I got fed up with always being able to have anything I wanted. I still got depressed and had to readjust to not having all that money at my disposal when I got home, but it never lasted.

And it wasn't always the easy life. We had to go to Brixton Prison once. Parts of it were being renovated and we had to get in to test their security measures and see how easy it was to access the main prison. Dressed appropriately in workmen's gear, Mazher and I went to the building contractor's recruiting office and asked about jobs at the prison. The woman there asked us if we had ever done wire reinforcing, and we said we had. We hadn't, of course, but they obviously needed wire reinforcers and to get the job we would have said yes to anything they'd wanted done. Since I knew a bit about building, I did know what wire reinforcing was, generally speaking; whereas, Maz knew nothing. Nevertheless, we both got jobs, starting the following day. There were no background or security checks on us.

The foreman took us to the cells they were renovating and just left us to it, assuming we knew what we were doing because we had specifically been sent to do this work. We couldn't work together because he had put us in two different empty cells, so we couldn't help each other work out what to do.

There was all this iron wire in there, which I had seen on building sites, where, normally, it was put on the floor and covered with cement. This had to go on the walls, which had metal rods coming out of them. I had no idea how to get started or even how to cut it to size. I went to the cell next door and introduced myself to the fellow doing this wire reinforcing in there, asked him how he was getting on and casually mentioned that I hadn't done much of it before. He showed me how the wire had to be measured, cut with an angle grinder, threaded through the rods and tied in a certain way, and then the wall had to be sprayed with cement.

It was a laborious, exacting job that would leave very little opportunity for flitting off to find out information and get a story, but at least I could do it; Maz couldn't. When I went to 'his' cell to explain it all, he didn't even know what an angle grinder was, let alone how to use one. I had to go to the 'ganger', or foreman, and tell him Maz suffered with migraines that were brought on by lifting heavy weights, and he was feeling ill. He was then given the job of sweeping the landings and I was stuck with the heavy work!

I found it easy and I was actually quite good at it. Because I wanted to do a good job and not get thrown off the site, I worked hard and kept getting more and more work, which just made it more difficult for me to get out and see the rest of the place. We ended up being there for about two weeks, and it was bloody hard work!

Fortunately, there were breaks and prefabricated buildings out at the back where you could have a cigarette and a cup of tea. I would meet up with Maz there and he would be complaining about being tired. He was just *sweeping*! Anyway, we managed to work our way round the back of these buildings. Wire mesh fences had been put up to separate the site from the prisoners' yard and we hung around there when the prisoners were out, until we struck up conversations with a few of them. Before long, they were asking us to get dope for them and pass it through. We didn't do that but we could have. Instead, we passed cigarettes through to them every lunchtime, and they were always happy to see us.

We got pictures of all that, and the story that ran was how easily we had got jobs inside Brixton Prison, been given security passes, were never searched and then had access to the inmates. We could have given them drugs, weapons - anything. It's all different now because security is much tighter everywhere, but not then. *News of the World* was very pleased with that story.

When it came out we assumed the contractors would work out that we were behind it because we just stopped going to the job, but they didn't. We actually got paid, and I got a note offering me a full time job, because I'd been such a good worker, and giving the name and number of whom to contact!

Working for *News of the World* sounds exciting, and it was, but it was not a continual succession of big stories, high life, good eating and hobnobbing with celebrities. And the continual emphasis on sex got boring.

Many a time, I had to get fillers for the paper, which often meant I had to go to a brothel that was masquerading as a sauna or a massage parlour, and expose them for what they were. I did two or three a week sometimes because they were quick. A typical example would be a massage parlour, where I'd sit in the waiting room with a couple of other fellows; there would be music playing and lots of magazines. The first fellow would go in and come out; the second fellow would go in and come out. Then I would go in and take everything off except my underwear, which was my chastity belt - if I had taken that off, it would have been tantamount to asking for sex. I would lie face down, and while she was doing the massage, she'd ask if there was anything else I needed. I'd ask her if she did 'extras', she'd ask what sort, and I'd ask if she 'took it up the bum'. She would say something to the effect that she might if I gave her fifty pounds. I would agree to her price, and then she would tell me to turn over onto my back. At that point, I would jump up and cower in the corner, saying I couldn't do it. I'd literally cry sometimes and act hysterical. She would be surprised by this behaviour, which gave me time to get my clothes back on, throw the money at her and run out. That was the only way to do it because as soon as she put her hands on me, sexually, she could say I was a client.

I went from terror, in the first brothel I went into when I was a plumber fixing the toilet, to boredom in the end. And it got on my nerves. What's the big deal about prostitutes? We know they shag for money. It's been going on since time immemorial.

No one does those kinds of stories any longer because they're not sensational enough but, then, they were the meat and gravy of *News of the World*; they are what made it so successful.

It was the same with wife swapping and sex parties: at first, I loved the excitement of being in a situation where everything was happening and I had to get pictures; then it all became the norm. I got so fed up I just wanted to go home. We went to so many filthy dirty dumps, pubs or inns, where an owner or manager had arranged a private sex party. I always had a girl with me and we posed as a couple, had drinks and hired a room for the night, because that was what was expected. It was always a long, tedious night because we'd have to get there about 8pm and fend everybody off for hours. We also always stayed fully dressed and many were the times we were questioned about that. Our continual plea or excuse was shyness and that this was our first time.

Generally speaking, you would expect people to go upstairs to have sex, but they often did it in front of everybody. That was no good to me because there were certain things that could not be shown, so I had to pick the right moments and watch for the more 'appropriate' shots. Cameras were never allowed, of course, and there could be no setting a picture up, or clicking away, taking endless shots to get the right one; it had to be very quick, but I always managed to get the pictures, which is why the paper always sent me. I brought it on myself. If I'd messed up a few jobs, they wouldn't have sent me so often.

For the same reason, I was sent to get pictures of paedophiles when the paper had the evidence but needed a picture. I don't remember most of those instances now, but, on one occasion, I was sent to get a picture of a guy who used to sell under-the-counter pornographic videos in his shop in Leytonstone. The shop was on the corner of a main road and there was roadwork going on, so I couldn't park anywhere to wait for an opportunity. I knocked on a door opposite, and an old lady answered. It was a long shot, but I said I was watching for drug dealers and asked if I could use her window. I expected her to ask for ID or shut the door in my face, but she just let me in and actually made me tea.

I waited a few hours. With no sight of this guy, I was getting very bored so I decided to give him a reason to come outside. I rang the shop and said I was from the council, calling about the roadwork. He complained, saying it was 'bloody noisy' and wanting to know when it would be finished. I said that that was what I was calling about, and wondered if he would do me a favour and give the guys a message because I couldn't get hold of them. (Mobile phones were not in general use then.) Would he tell them that they had to work Saturday and Sunday to finish the job? He, of course, agreed and put the phone down. Next thing, he came out of the shop and yelled this message to the workers. They just told him to 'fuck off', and I got my pictures.

# 18
# Bosnia

April 1993

It was the month when the IRA blew up the City of London. There was only one person killed: Ed Henty, a photographer, and if I had been in London, that would have been me. I was in Bosnia, and Ed was doing my shift that Saturday.

It was unusual for the *News of the World* to ask me to go to Bosnia, and even Stuart White - the journalist I went with - thought so. 'If there are good stories out there, they probably think we'll get them with you,' he concluded. I appreciated the compliment.

We flew to Split, in Croatia, and booked into a hotel. Because we were going into a war zone, our first call was to register with NATO and get special Press Passes. It was surreal: one minute we were preparing to go into a war zone and the next we were eating venison in a beautiful restaurant in Split, where it was blissfully quiet, and the people lovely.

On day two, we enquired about renting a vehicle to go to the town of Vitez in Bosnia, not far from Sareyevo, and soon discovered that there were none: you had to buy instead of rent because you might get blown up and the car would be gone.

We looked around, debating what to do. The BBC and *Daily Mail* were also in Split, and, although they were not going to Vitez, we noticed that they had armoured cars, which were ordinary cars made bullet proof (supposedly) by a local entrepreneur, who was making a fortune out of them. They cost about three thousand pounds, so I rang up the managing editor to get the go ahead to buy one. He refused. We had to buy a soft-skinned vehicle, so we bought an old Skoda, but then could not insure it for the same reason we could not rent a vehicle – the high risk factor.

Once we had a car, we tried to hire a guide; no one wanted the job. They never said why, but they might have thought that if we could not afford an armoured vehicle, we probably could not afford to pay them. And/or, it might have been because we were going in a soft-skinned vehicle – that risk factor again!

It was only a thirty or forty mile trip, but we were told it would take between twelve and twenty four hours because the roads had been, and were being bombed, and there were snipers, all making it very difficult and dangerous. They suggested a route through the mountains, which was marginally less dangerous, and told us to stock up with spirits and cigarettes to give to the rebels. We did all that, got a pencilled map from somebody, and off we went. We should have refused to go but we didn't because we were young and stupid.

It was a hair-raising, horrendous journey. There were no purpose-built roads, just old donkey tracks. In some parts, there was a sheer drop on one side; and there were frequent blockages caused by exploded trees that we had to go round or get out and move. The going was so slow that we had to stop three quarters of the way up the mountain and sleep the night in the car; it was *freezing* cold.

We woke up to a beautiful, crisp, sunny day and, eventually, reached a clearing at the top of the mountain. The views were stunning: lakes, encircled by mountains, reflected perfectly blue sky. It was peaceful - absolutely lovely - giving no hint of the horrific scenes not far away.

We began the drive down and after about half an hour, we could hear rumblings: two NATO tanks were coming towards us, filling the width of the road. With no room to get past them or turn round, we had to back up the mountain. Thankfully, after about a mile, there was a small space where we could turn round, and we carried on, facing forward, back up to the top.

The guys in the tanks happened to be English and we chatted to them for a bit. In their opinion, we were mad to be doing this, and besides, Vitez was bombed out; there was nothing much left but an army base.

Regardless, we carried on down the side of the mountain and came to a barrier, manned by three men with guns. They asked us where we were going; we told them and thought they would lift the barrier, but they didn't, they just stood there. Then we realised what they were waiting for: we gave them whisky and cigarettes, and they let us through, one of them pointing to his head as if to say 'mad English', and we were!

We got down into the town and saw that a water main had been fractured. These people were desperate for water and there it was, just spurting out of this pipe. Having been trained as a plumber years before, I knew it was a simple thing to fix. I got two bricks and hit both sides of the pipe to bend the lead across the hole and close it; that slowed the spurt to a drip.

When I got back in the car, we soon found out why nobody had bothered to fix it before: we drove past a car that had the windows open and everything dissolved into slow motion as we heard the zing of a bullet – somebody was firing at us. We tried to go faster but we couldn't because we had to avoid a lot of debris that was in the road from the bombed houses. We did soon manage to drive round a bend though. There was a dead donkey there with its stomach hanging out, stinking and covered with flies; then, further down the road, the bodies of a woman and a headless child. The woman looked like she had been crawling towards the baby and had been shot in the back of the head trying to reach it. We were shocked and scared, but had to stop the car because we were both violently sick. I had seen horrible things before and they had upset me but I could usually contain it. Not this time. It still affects me now.

We carried on; the road was littered with bodies, some of them squashed and appearing to sit up because tanks had gone over the body and crushed the bones flat, but not the head. Nobody had cleared them away or buried them because they would have been dead, too, if they had . That was our introduction to Bosnia. It makes me feel ill, remembering it.

We got to a village where there were a couple of people from the *Daily Mail*. One girl wasn't well; she'd seen all that we had seen and she couldn't get over it. We asked them where they were billeted because there were no hotels, obviously, and people were billeting wherever they could. They told us we would have to knock on somebody's door and offer them money to put us up.

We went to a farmhouse and an elderly lady answered the door; she couldn't speak English, but she knew why we were there. She was extremely poor. The roof and part of the farmhouse had been blasted away, and they had put a makeshift tarpaulin over it. Even that had holes in it. It was a mess and I don't know why we picked that one - there were other houses that still had roofs - except that they obviously needed money. We gave her some, and then her ageing husband came in carrying an old-fashioned, First World War, bolt action gun with a bayonet on it; he was indicating that he'd protect us. Maria and Adil were lovely people.

It was freezing cold in the farmhouse, despite the fire they had going; there was no adequate way to heat a building with no roof. We knew we would only be there for a week or two, but they were *living* there. They'd had a normal life like the rest of us, and it had been blown apart.

Maria cooked us scrambled eggs, and served them up with some bread. We thanked her and ate it, not realising that she had only had four eggs and given us two of them. We had given her money, which wasn't much use when there was nothing to buy; yet, she had still shared what little she had with us. In the days following, she also washed all our clothes down at a stream and ironed them with hot bricks. I don't know how she did it, but she kept us looking smart.

All the first day, it was very quiet: no bombs, no bullets, nothing. We went to sleep wondering about that, only to be woken, all of sudden, by an anti-aircraft gun continuously firing. I got up and looked out. Two or three farms away, somebody was firing tracer bullets, which are red, so you can see them. We managed to work out from Adil and Maria that this was the postman, who hated the other side and did this every night. I was trying to explain that this was stupid because the other side could see where the bullets were coming from, but they already knew that.

We ran along to the postman, trying to explain to him that what he was doing was insane, but he just told us to get away, or words to that effect. Then he stopped firing. It was pitch black and we heard 'ping, ping, ping': the other side was firing back at him but hitting everything else, and the shells were huge, glowing red because they were so hot. We could see them, and the other side could see where they were going and move around accordingly. They couldn't see us so we ran as fast as we could!

The second day in Bosnia, we went to the army base and asked if we could go out with them on one of their sorties in their armoured vehicles. They were not very helpful because they had a job to do and we were in the way. I had a laugh and a joke with the sergeant and managed to get a bit of a rapport going before we went back to the farmhouse, wondering what to do next. We knew it was ridiculously dangerous for us to go out in our own

241

soft-skin car. Even if we had, not being able to speak the language meant we couldn't communicate with anyone local. We decided to go and find some food instead.

The *Daily Mail* had tins of this, tins of that, powdered eggs - all well prepared. They were girls! They would have! We had laughed at them, but we were the ones starving. They gave us some powdered egg, which we had to say was nice but tasted like cow's intestine. We were glad of it, though.

We were still very hungry, however, so I decided to go back to the army base and get some beer and some more food, if I could. It was after dark by this time, and I decided not to go in the car because it would have made too much noise. Then, as I was walking, I began to think I was being a bit stupid because it was pitch black and I couldn't see anything but the stars. There was only one road - I couldn't get lost - but I'd been told not to use a torch or even light a cigarette because snipers would see the glow.

'Stay where you are! Put your hands up!' somebody suddenly said in English.

I put my hands up, and, within seconds, two or three soldiers were round me. They had 'night sights' on so they could see me.

'I'm a journalist,' I told them.

'Only a stupid journalist would walk in the dark where there are snipers!' one of the soldiers remarked.

*He's got a point!* I thought, as they took me back to the base. I *was* reckless.

'What the fuck are you doing here?!' The sergeant was more than a little surprised to see me. 'You're bloody *mad*!' he erupted.

'I know, but I just came to see if you'd give us some food and beer. We're absolutely starving,' I explained.

'You can't eat in the barracks!'

'Why not?'

'It's against army rules - for *your* safety,' he explained. 'The barracks could be bombed and you could get killed. We'll give you some food to take back to your billet, though. The beer, you'll have to pay for.'

I had walked there safely, so I should be safe to walk back, apparently. I decided not to push my luck by asking for a lift. They piled up so much stuff, I couldn't carry it all, so I just took the beer and some tins of sardines in olive oil and left most of it to come back for the next day.

Stuart and I ate the sardines, including the olive oil because I remembered my mother saying you should do that. Well, they came straight out the other end of Stuart. He had the 'trots' - a stomach bug or something. The toilets had all been blown up so he was forever going and digging a hole, poor guy, until Maria gave him some liquid, which turned out to be pure charcoal. It worked though.

We got the rest of the food and beer the next day and shared it with Maria and Aldi. We had tins of processed chicken and Old Oak Ham, which we had to open with a Swiss Army knife, getting the jelly all over the place. Sardines and Old Oak Ham aren't bad together, actually!

We went back and forth to the barracks after that. We weren't supposed to go beyond the reception area, but I wheedled my way in. I got to know them and we had a good laugh, so they turned a blind eye to us going in at night and having a drink. And, finally, they invited us to meet them early one morning and go with them to a hospital to deliver supplies.

There were two armoured vehicles: one was carrying the supplies; the other was carrying soldiers to protect the supply vehicle and help unload at the other end. We were with the soldiers, and along the way I wanted to go to the toilet. Normally, they had a disposal mechanism, but they weren't using it in case a grenade had been hidden in it to blow us up. Someone suggested I go in a bucket, but the driver asked me not to because the vehicle was sealed and it would have stunk the place out. I was desperate so to take my mind off it he suggested I go up front and have a look at where we were going, which was back through Vitez. I could not believe it: there were so many more bodies than when we'd arrived; they were everywhere.

'We're going to have to be very careful,' he said. 'Usually, we go straight over the bodies because they're dead anyway. We daren't now. The rebels have started cutting open the stomachs, taking the intestines out, putting anti-personnel mines inside and turning them over so that the mines are hidden; when a tank goes over, up it goes.'

We went round to the side, knocking down small trees as we went. Looking out, I saw that the other vehicle wasn't doing the same, but going straight over the bodies. The drivers were talking to each other by radio.

'You're *insane*! There could be mines in there.'

'I'm not fucking around!' That driver was an idiot and said some unrepeatable things.

Despite all that, we got through safely and arrived at the local 'hospital'. It was a bombed building, formerly a school, and the makeshift hospital was in the basement. As we climbed out of the vehicle, a bullet hit the side of it. Everybody dived to the ground, and whenever somebody moved there was the loud ping of another bullet hitting the metal. The other vehicle had a sub-machine gun on top, and the soldiers started firing indiscriminately into the general area the bullets were coming from. It was a bigger vehicle than ours and the driver also pulled in front of us so that we could unload. We formed a chain and got the supplies into the 'hospital', which I was told was disgusting but all that the locals had. I decided to go and have a look.

On the operating table, there was a Serb who had been shot in the ear. A Bosnian soldier - supposedly a surgeon - with a bloodstained white coat over his uniform, was sewing up the Serb's ear, and the guy was screaming because they didn't have any anaesthetic. Presumably, we had just brought some. The fact that he was bleeding profusely may have been the reason they didn't stop to make him more comfortable. Although, considering what followed, I wonder. I took pictures of everything, including close-up pictures of the Serb, and then walked away. It was insensitive and I should not have done it, but when you're behind the lens you don't think about those things. I heard the Serb say something; a few seconds later, a gun was fired. I went back to find that they had shot him through the head. He was dead but his heart kept pumping blood that was shooting out of his head and making it move around in rhythm with the heartbeat. It kept on until there was no more blood.

I asked them why they had done that. They said he was the enemy, anyway, and he had called me a pig for taking his picture. Basically, he got shot because I took a picture of him. I think they would have shot him anyway, because they were all animals. Shooting him was nothing compared to what they did to women and children: the NATO soldiers told us that both sides put babies on bayonets and made the mothers watch them squirm before they died; then they killed the mothers.

Two soldiers opened a door, picked up the Serb and threw him in. They told me that was the mortuary. Of course, being me, I had to look. There must have been two or three dozen bodies – men, women and children - stacked up in a pile. Blood had drained down the sides and congealed. It was like a hideous Dali painting, and the smell was overwhelming. They were waiting for someone to come and take them away, but nobody ever did.

What got to me, were the kids – the babies. And that was all in the name of ethnicity and religion! Many more things happened and there were many more pictures, but they all told the same terrible horror story. There was a boy with no arms. They had pulled him like a Christmas cracker. He survived. The memory brings the emotions back, and I go hot and cold.

Everybody else had satellite to send pictures back; we didn't, and we had to borrow a satellite phone because the biggest paper in the world didn't have one of their own, equipment not being high on *News of the World*'s agenda. They had given us a very modern computer, but where were we going to get the electricity to run it? And how were we to get a BT line in Kosovo?! We had *nothing*. Because of the friends I had made, we went to the army base and they let me transmit back to England.

While we were doing that, we heard that the IRA had blown up the City with a massive lorry bomb. The area had been cleared by the police beforehand, and nobody knows how or why Ed Henty was there, or why the police hadn't seen him. He had a family, and he was not the type of person who would have been doing something reckless to get a picture. *News of the World* gave his wife a paltry hundred thousand pounds in compensation. They sent flowers to the funeral and she tore them up.

Obviously, that Sunday, the bombing was a much bigger story than Bosnia. After all the chances we had taken and all that we had seen, the story was never used. Why *News of the World* risked our lives by sending us in the first place, I don't know. I knew that the pictures would never be published, anyway, because they weren't *News of the World*'s style; nevertheless, it had been my job to take them.

When we were coming back, the price of petrol had risen to fifty pounds a gallon, and the paper gave us an argument about paying it. I was so incensed. What did that matter after all that I had seen? Then we had difficulty getting a regular flight back. As I sat in a tiny seat in a freezing cold freight plane, my time in Bosnia really began to hit home. There were some female army personnel on the plane, coming home for medical reasons, and we all got totally drunk. When we landed, we were de-briefed, after which I got totally drunk again. The mini-cab driver, who always came to pick me up, could see the state I was in but took me anyway. I was sick inside and outside his car. All I said to Jeannette was 'hello'. I was put to bed and I didn't talk to her until the next morning. And I *stunk*! There had been no way to wash properly in Bosnia.

The whole experience had a very bad effect on me, emotionally. I'll never ever forget it. I was off work for weeks, genuinely ill. I drank twice as much and smoked twice as much. Anger and grief had hardened me and made me see life totally differently: nothing was the same anymore. Until you've been somewhere like that - seen the children and the women, seen them killed for absolutely no reason whatsoever - you can never ever know the *suffering*. Forget the bodies, they're dead; it's the people left behind who suffer. Apart from the terror and the grief and the trauma, everyday life becomes a burden. I saw people, whose lives had been as normal as ours, digging in the ground because there was *no* fresh water; they had to dig and dig and dig until, eventually, they found some and could survive another day. When we first went there, we were looking for the tap and the soap and the bum paper, but it was no longer the same world as the one we had come from. And for what? So called religion that allows people to die, with nobody caring unless it's happening to them.

I used to be the same: I would hear about something happening far away and not think much about it. I was earning good money; we had a good life, meeting stars, doing anything we wanted, and Bosnia made me realise I had been complacent. That realisation has never left me.

When I first went back to work, I could not handle it. I argued with people. I thought everything was a load of crap, and I didn't know what I was doing here any more. I could no longer understand why we were doing the usual stuff; it had become stupid and immaterial to me. It was like being on drugs: staring into space while everything was going in, and thinking how pointless it all was. At a dinner party or some such gathering, I'd look at my watch and think, *that's half an hour of my life gone while that person is talking a load of garbage.* We can't all be clever and talk about deep things all the time, but we don't have to talk sheer rubbish! I would get angry and have to excuse myself and leave.

I was so angry I wanted to go back to Bosnia and help, get back into the thick of it and then maybe I'd be sane: I'd see all the killing and the babies crying and be back in real life. Of course, everyone told me, and I realised for myself, that there was nothing I could do for those people. I just thought maybe that was what I was meant for: to photograph all those kinds of things and open people's eyes. We're so cosseted, so protected. Everything we do is trivial.

A year later, working to take care of the family and make a better life, everything still seemed futile and meaningless to me. If Jeannette wanted me to go with her to Oxford Street, all I saw were countless people walking around aimlessly, doing nothing but buying things they would put in a skip two months later, all of them talking about what they'd bought or what they were doing in their own little lives. I hated it, and I hated Christmas for the same reason. *What a waste of life!* Not to them, of course! It was all very important to them. But it *is* a waste of life. I still think so. What are they doing? They don't know what life is. We're all total mugs. Our service personnel go off to fight and we wave them goodbye; they come back and we might wave again. Then they're forgotten. Those same men and women, maimed emotionally and/or physically, may not find jobs, may struggle, but they are forgotten. It's the same now as it ever was: nobody wants to see life's sores; they only want to see the good parts.

I don't know if it made me a better person but I appreciate everything now because nothing is for very long; it's all temporary. I can never walk away from trouble either. If two people were walking towards me looking menacing, I might be terrified but I could not turn and expose my back. Even if they might kill me, I would still have to keep going because it would feel so real. Everything I do now is immaterial by comparison with Bosnia.

After what I have seen over the years, whatever life throws at me will not be half as bad as what I've seen already. That is why I want my life to be as full as possible, and why I believe in living life for today and not worrying about what tomorrow might bring. You've only got one life, and you're a long time dead: that has stopped being a cliché for me and become very real. Whatever I want to do or have, I go for it *now*, or at least I try. I don't fuck around. Bosnia showed me that it's just as the pathologist said: we're like automatons; the heart is a machine and when the batteries run out, you're dead and that's the end of it. The Serb who got shot in the head was here one minute and gone the next. I could drop dead tomorrow. That's why, with every breath you take, you have to *live*. When you wake up in the morning, be thankful you're alive; put your feet on the floor and get out there and do something. You know you're going to die, but you don't know when, so don't put anything off: *enjoy* life while you can.

When you die, you may not be forgotten, but it doesn't take long before the tears are over and everyone gets on with their life. And that's how it should be, because that's Nature's way. To think you might go somewhere else after you die would be lovely, I guess, but, from what I've seen, I don't believe in God at all, and I don't believe there's anything after death. Heaven and hell make a very good story, and every religion is a different rendition of the same thing, but it's the stuff of nonsense as far as I'm concerned. Maybe it helps people when they're dying, and I'll probably clutch at straws too, and say 'Please, God!' when it's my turn. But how can you believe in a God who can do miracles but gives us free will and doesn't interfere when someone puts a baby on the end of a bayonet, simply because it's from another religion or ethnic group, and watches it squirm while it dies? Other people think that those who do that don't deserve to live, so they kill them, and on and on it goes. There's no settling any of it, but people believe in a God who lets that happen.

I developed Crohn's disease. After I held on and didn't go to the toilet in the armoured vehicle, the feeling went. I did not actually go for a month and the pain was terrible. I was prescribed all kinds of laxatives and suppositories and eventually everything seemed all right. But it wasn't: I started getting awful pain again. I kept going to the doctor but it just got worse and worse. For a long time, no one knew what the problem was. Then the doctors concluded that holding everything in caused something to happen to my metabolism, which led to the collapse of my intestines, and they operated. I'm now on medication and B12 injections for the rest of my life.

It was all the result of my experiences in Bosnia. I'm not a hero or a clever man, but I wasn't frightened when I was *in* Bosnia. At the time, I thought I was being brave, not feeling or showing fear because it would stop me from doing what I wanted or needed to do; in fact, all the fear was being repressed in my subconscious and going to my stomach; it was all registering in my body instead of my mind, and it was only afterwards that I kept wondering, *why did I do that?*

# 19

# For Mickey

Early in 1997, not knowing that, later in the year, the shit was due to hit the fan and turn my life upside down yet again, I was on an investigation that really amused me. It was with a very likeable rogue I knew, Michael McNamee, or Mickey as he was commonly called.

There was a big art theft from a gallery in Bond Street and Mickey rang me one morning about 2am to tell me he knew the guys who had carried out the robbery. He stressed that he had had nothing to do with the robbery, itself, and did not have any idea where the thieves were hiding. He had simply received a call from one of them, saying they wanted to blackmail the insurance company into paying for the return of the art, or they would burn it. They wanted Mickey to liase with the newspapers and get them to set up the deal with the insurance company.

We arranged to meet the following evening and, as we walked down Bond Street, chatting, Mickey abruptly stopped, took a set of keys from his pocket and proceeded to unlock a door at the side of the gallery that had been robbed.

'What the fuck are you doing?' I asked, panicking as he opened the door and the alarm went off.

'Don't worry. I've got the code for the alarm,' he said, pressing the appropriate numbers.

Walking up the stairs to the first floor, Mickey opened a door that led into a toilet. Closing it behind us, he proceeded towards the toilet pan.

'What are we doing in here? Are you going to have a piss?' I was bewildered.

'No. Just hold on a minute,' he said, taking a screwdriver out of his pocket this time. He began to unscrew the panel that concealed the cistern at the back of the toilet pan, by which time, sweat was pouring down my face and to say I was a tad nervous would be a gross understatement. Mickey lifted off the panel to reveal several works of art and took out a couple of the paintings.

'Is this the stolen art from the gallery downstairs?' I asked, redundantly. As if it could it be anything else!

'Of course it is!' Mickey replied.

The thieves had never taken the art out of the building!

Mickey pointed to a small painting of Napoleon with his hands clasped behind his back, looking out from the cliffs of Elba. 'You can have this one, if you want, Mate,' he offered. 'It's only a small one.'

That was typical of Mickey: a loveable rogue, always trying to help everybody, with a possible jail sentence thrown in for good measure!

Roger Insall and I worked on the story and got in touch with the insurance company, but no deal was ever made as the insurance company, understandably, refused to be blackmailed.

Mickey died recently of liver cancer. When he rang, he always brought a smile to my face and he will be sadly missed. May his God go with him.

I did not, by the way, take him up on his offer of the painting.

# 20
# The Beast

In the autumn of 1997, I was asked to go to Bodmin Moor with a young freelance reporter, Graham Johnson, and his colleague Ricky Sutton, to look for the 'Beast of Bodmin', which is supposed to be some kind of panther. I thought it strange and suggested they send a junior photographer. I was then told that Rebekah Wade, the Deputy Editor, had requested me. I didn't know it, but apparently she was planning a series about this type of thing to impress Rupert Murdoch.

We went to Cornwall and did the usual thing: Graham and Ricky talked to people who claimed to have seen the 'Beast', but it was a 'no go' story and a load of rubbish as far as I was concerned. I was just biding my time, waiting for them to tell us to come back home.

We were doing the story 'tongue in cheek', based on *The Hound of the Baskervilles*, as instructed: Graham and Ricky had dressed up as Sherlock Holmes and Doctor Watson, and I had taken pictures of them looking at trees with magnifying glasses, as if they're asking, 'Is this the Beast of Bodmin Moor?' Ricky was then called back to London and he took the films with him. After that, Ray Levine, the Features Editor, called Graham and told him the pictures were too frivolous. Over the course of several more calls, Graham felt so pressured to get a picture of the 'Beast' that he felt his job was on the line. These calls were not made by Rebekah Wade, herself, but I believed they were made at her instigation, and she was not someone I could tell to 'fuck off'. I also wanted to help Graham, so, after much discussion, we went to a wildlife park and I took some pictures of a puma at an angle that made it look much bigger than it was – all very obvious, we thought. We still believed the piece was supposed to be light-hearted, and we sent the pictures in, imagining they'd all have a laugh back at the paper. This was my first big mistake.

Wade called to congratulate me on the pictures and she was with Stuart Kuttner, the Managing Editor, who wanted to add his congratulations. He asked me if the pictures were genuine. I was stunned. How could they not see they were a joke? I had to make an instant decision. I was not the only one involved and I did not want to betray my colleagues - principally Rebekah Wade - by explaining to Kuttner about the phone calls to Graham and the pressure he had felt. I made my second big mistake and said the pictures were genuine.

I returned to London the next day and the whole thing just escalated out of control. There were plans to cover the first six pages of the paper with this 'big scoop'. In the end, I left the office to think things through and went out for dinner with Jeannette. I knew I couldn't let the situation continue, but I needed some space. While we were out, Mazher Mahmood rang my mobile and questioned me about the story, telling me that Wade really did think it was genuine. I couldn't believe it, and because Maz was someone I considered a friend, I spoke openly about the whole situation. I told him I would call Wade when I got home.

I don't know for a fact that he taped the conversation, but I assume he did because he went straight to Wade and, for reasons best known to himself, told her the story was all a big set-up. Not knowing what he was up to, I rang Rebekah Wade myself, as soon as I got home, and put my hands up to it. Of course, she already knew. She didn't mention Maz's name, but he was the only person I had spoken to about it.

I admitted it was a stupid thing for someone of my experience to do, but as newspaper people they must all have seen it was a pile of rubbish and meant as a joke. She said she had taken it seriously because I had sent it in as a real story, and she denied putting any pressure on Graham and me, through Ray Levine, to get it; she was smart enough to know I'd be taping the call. By then, it had all gone too far, anyway, because the pages were set up to go to press and the Executive Chairman had been told we had this massive story.

After I put that call in, Stuart Kuttner, the Managing Editor, rang and said he wanted me to come down to the office right away to meet with him and Wade. It must have been close to midnight when I drove to Wapping. There was a conversation, and I was suspended.

I could not believe this was happening to me. Within days, there was a dismissal hearing and I was fired for gross misconduct. I was so shocked, I took *News of the World* to court for wrongful dismissal, which was a silly thing to do and my third big mistake. I was one man against this huge organisation.

I did it because of my principles and because I wanted my name back. I was Senior Investigations Photographer with - until that point – a good reputation on the paper and a much wider remit than taking photographs: I was involved in surveillance and the use of highly sophisticated equipment - responsibilities which were authorised by the Editor and only given to a few people. I had no need to stunt up pictures for my own benefit, and certainly not for a story I considered rubbish from the start. I *had* done wrong, but I'd told the truth about a story before publication. I felt like the sacrificial lamb, paying for Wade's mistakes.

My barrister was basing my case on what he called 'a culture of fabrication' at *News of the World*, in which mocked up stories were not unusual. In the desperation of the moment, trying to build my case and get evidence, I rang colleagues at the paper, starting at an outer periphery of those involved, working my way in, gathering incriminating information, and, unbeknownst to them, taping every conversation.

I'm not proud of that. I used to be a nice person. But I wasn't going to sit there and let them do this to me. I knew all the tricks, I knew what was going on, and the majority of them deserved to be turned over because they were doing the same to me.

From day one, my so-called friends were like frozen water, melting away. Some things, I expected, like the possibility that my house was bugged; others, I didn't, like the time I went for a drink with a mate and ended up being threatened with legal action. A reporter I thought was a good friend invited me to go for a drink for the express purpose of turning me over. (He shall remain nameless because he has since died and cannot defend himself.) He was freelance at the time, and because his family had originally come from the same part of the world as mine and I liked him, I'd helped him get work. We sat chatting, having a laugh and a joke, and then I realised it was a set-up because he kept going to the toilet at very regular intervals. If he had been drinking beer, I might have put it down to a weak bladder, but he was drinking shorts, so I realised he was taping me and going into the toilets to change or check the tapes. More than once, he asked me for Mazher Mahmood's address, which I refused to give because, obviously, I wouldn't give out personal details, plus I knew he must already have it. He asked me again, as we were leaving the pub, and I said 'Yeah, I'll give it to you for your birthday'. (Another joke! I have to stop making them!)

A couple of hours later, about 1.30am - after he'd taken the tape back to the office and they'd listened to it, a letter from Stuart Kuttner was hand delivered to my house, threatening legal action if I made Mazher Mahmood's address public and compromised his safety as an investigative journalist exposing criminals. All that was on the tape was my refusal to give his personal details, except for the wise-crack at the end. The letter was just to wind me up and show how powerful they were; it was harassment because they wanted me to shut up, and I wouldn't. But in the process, I learned that my 'friends' were just colleagues, trying to get a step up on the ladder.

Unfortunately, acting out of desperation was like throwing in a grenade and innocent people getting hurt: I didn't pick and choose; I taped everybody. Stuart White, who was in Bosnia with me, did not deserve it. My barrister later used the taped conversations as evidence at the tribunal, and Stuart had said a lot. He didn't get fired, but it landed him in the shit with the paper, and I did tell him how sorry I was. I had done him such an injustice. I still am sorry. I should have stopped the barrister from using that particular tape. Being sorry doesn't change things, of course, but I do regret the hurt I caused.

The case did not come to court for nearly a year, a very bad year for Jeannette, as well as me. After all the ups and downs of business in the past, including bankruptcy, she had been happy that I had a good job, earning a lot of money even by today's standards, and had the security of a good pension. I was pretty much at the top of the tree, and she was angry with me and very bitter that I had lost it all because of something so stupid. She did not want me to take it to court, and neither did a really good friend, Roger Hull, who was an ex-copper and had been through something similar. He said, 'Steve, just take it on the chin. Don't be bitter.' They both strongly advised against it, and I should have listened, but I was determined. The bastards had turned on me and I felt I had to do it. It caused a lot of arguments between Jeannette and I, and many a marriage would probably have broken down under the strain; it was a terrible cloud hanging over us, and it dragged on for so long. Happily, ours didn't, which may be due to the fact that Jeannette says I'm a lot nicer, much better person, when we don't have anything!

Truth to tell, I was getting bored with my job at *News of the World*. I had done it all so many times I could do it in my sleep. *But,* losing it the way I did, and the disgrace of it, was worse than losing a family member. When it happened, I had a hollow, sick, inner desperation: the feeling of, *I don't care if I die. If I die today, good, because that would be the easiest thing for me.* I couldn't see a way out. When things are not that bad, I can think ahead. But when they're *really* terrible my brain gets so cluttered I can't think. That's when the bad feelings about being dyslexic crowd in and I think I'm not a clever person; I'm just an idiot. Although the bankruptcy was truly terrible, I was younger then and, at the end of the day, it was only money. This time, I had lost much more and thought I could never get it back: professional standing and respect. I don't know *how* I got through it. There was nothing to help me except my belief that you have got to get up and get on with things, because you're a long time dead.

Nobody would give me a job in the Press. I was like a leper. *News of the World* has a long reach, and no one wanted anything from me to rub off on them. It wasn't easy taking rejection again and again, ringing people I thought were my friends and continually hearing: 'Sorry Steve, there's nothing at the moment.'

The money we had had in reserve was disappearing fast, and I started doing anything I could think of, including cleaning windows and doing an early morning sandwich round at building sites. Jeannette was working and doing overtime, so I was often the chief cook and bottle washer at home, which was a new experience for me, but I think I did all right. In the end, I got a plumbing job with a company called *Power Rod*. They did all the dirty jobs at the lower end of the market: fixing broken toilets in bookmakers, after people had smashed them because they'd lost bets; cleaning drains; going into filthy houses with blocked toilets and a stench that was indescribable.

It showed me how far I'd come from the high life: after nights at the Savoy, big receptions and dinners with stars, I was unblocking toilets. But *Power Rod* did me a favour because the job helped me get back into plumbing, until I could get back into the Press. I couldn't have gone into a high-end company because I wouldn't have been able to do the work. I had to start again, like I had done years before, cleaning drains.

It upset me for the first few weeks and I don't know how I stood it. I didn't want anyone to see me. When they sent me to the West End, I wore a cap, pulled right down over my face, because I had to go to places where I'd been as a journalist. One was the Oxo Building, where there's a beautiful restaurant. I was cleaning out a blocked toilet and I could hear two blokes talking while they were washing their hands. One of them was a journalist from the *Daily Mirror*, and he would have known me. I locked myself in the toilet and hid until he'd gone. Even then, I was really scared I'd walk out and be seen.

We had to work all the hours that God sends – 9am until 10 or 11pm - to make about four hundred pounds a week. I just couldn't physically work all those hours, so I was only getting about two hundred. It was terrible, but I had to get on with it. I did a bit of ducking and diving and took pictures when I could. But then, when I tried to sell them, nobody would buy them.

On the day the case went to court, *News of the World* offered to settle, on condition I didn't publish anything; but, on the advice of my barrister, I refused. I was completely stressed out and in no frame of mind to be making decisions, plus I was paying for advice I assumed was good, so I took it. With hindsight, I should have taken the settlement. So much for expensive advice!

By this time, we had no money, nobody wanted to talk to me, and I felt very much on my own. The only boost I got was from a couple of articles in the now defunct Punch magazine. The first article (1-13 August, 1998) was headlined: GRAYSON FAVOURED TO TURN SCREWS ON RAG. Beside a picture of a judge's gavel coming down on the words NEWS OF THE WORLD, was a short humorous piece beginning: Legal eagles are excited about an East London industrial tribunal which promises to be compelling.

At the risk of blowing my own trumpet, it mentioned my 'exemplary reputation for investigative work' and my delivery of 'scoop after scoop'. I only include these comments here because they meant so much to me at a time when I felt that any success I had previously achieved had been erased.

This was followed by another article (12-25 September, 1998), written by John McVicar once the case was underway. His take on the whole sorry idea of the Beast of Bodmin Moor was the same as mine:

If it was Cornwall's answer to the Nessie, Bigfoot, the Yeti and corn circles, it hasn't turned into much of a tourist attraction because its natural habitat seems to be the middle pages of tabloids rather than the moors of Cornwall. It's a silly-season spread which usually features a morphed Tiddles or a blurred snap of a wildlife park's big cat.

Of Rebekah Wade, he wrote:

Most of the two days was spent listening to a very uncomfortable Wade denying that the Screws [*News of the World*] ever trafficked in stunted-up stories. She told the court, without even a hint of a smile: "The whole ideology of the *News of the World* is based on truth."… she blinked and hand-wrestled her spindly fingers as she denied, denied and denied.

I did not know the outcome of the court case for a long time; the decision was ages coming through. I can still picture exactly where I was when the solicitor rang to say we'd lost: I was doing a job outside London, fixing a main that had burst. I went absolutely numb, finished the job, and then went and sat in the van, thinking it was all over. At that moment, I didn't believe I'd ever get back into the newspaper trade. Even though I had known we probably wouldn't win, it was still a terrible shock and I was very bitter. My mistake hadn't been the Beast of Bodmin story; my mistake had been taking a newspaper like *News of the World* to court. I lost so much and to add insult to injury I had to work the evening shift after that, as well!

Lots of people rang me to say how sorry they were after reading the decision in the paper. Before long, my solicitor also rang again. I did not have to pay all the costs for both sides, but there were huge bills: his and the barrister's. I owed a lot of money – tens of thousands of pounds - and I didn't have it. They had been lovely people who believed in me; now they were threatening to take me to court. It couldn't be helped; that's the system. I had to give them a statement of earnings and outgoings and pay them bit by bit, until we sold the house.

It was the same scenario as the bankruptcy all over again: struggling and having to sell our house to pay off huge debts. Fortunately, we sold both properties when the market was good and made enough money to pay everything off. But it was so sad when we walked out of the house in Hatch End. It had been a dump when we bought it, smelling strongly of dog. And the problems were not only cosmetic: all the lights went one day and when John, my electrician friend, took a look behind the walls, he found that it had been wired wrongly and all the wires were hot; the previous owner had obviously done it all himself.

We gutted the place and lived in one room while everything was re-done. We made it beautiful: I had a study full of books and gold discs that *Abbey Road Studios* had given me; Jeannette had a huge dressing room where I'd built floor to ceiling cupboards and a dressing table, all myself, by hand; there was a full-length mirror with lights all around it, and lots of special little things like well-placed plugs for her hair dryer and so on. It was very hard, losing all that we'd built up for the second time.

We had to rent a flat for a few months before we moved into the house we have now. It's a new two-bedroom house with more bathrooms and toilets than rooms! It's just somewhere to live. I don't think I'll ever be happy there; it's not my home; it's not where I belong.

After working for *Power Rod* for a while, I got a job with *Pimlico Plumbers,* which was at the high end of the market. I told the boss, Charlie Mullins, that I had been a plumber, years ago, and had recently worked for *Power Rod,* but that I was a journalist. I made this clear because, even though I was still a pariah in the newspaper business, I intended to get back into it and did not expect to be plumbing for long.

Charlie was good to me and if it wasn't for him I don't know what I would have done. I think he liked the fact that I was a little bit different, and I liked the fact that I always knew where I stood with him. He gave me a job and a van and I went from earning two shillings a week to an average of three thousand pounds a week. He was soon sending me on call-outs because I'm a good talker and I could get the work. One job I got in Kensington took five or six workers and lasted for six months because we had to gut the whole house. I would get jobs like that all the time, so I was earning a fortune and so was *Pimlico Plumbers.*

At the same time, I was always doing any other bits and pieces I could get, like investigations for the *Mirror,* or whoever asked me. People I knew would ring me up and I would investigate things for them in the evenings, after doing plumbing work during the day. Everyone at *Pimlico* knew I was an investigator and a journalist - different from the usual plumber. Because of that, they did things to wind me up sometimes, but it was all in good fun. I love *Madam Butterfly* and they would regularly take my tape out of the van and set the radio to hip-hop stations. I would be driving along, trying to find something I could listen to, and all this 'boom-boom' *noise* would be coming at me, which I couldn't get rid of.

After a while, I started getting pains in my hands and I couldn't do the work. I thought I would have to leave, but Charlie came up with the idea of making me a supervisor. That way, I still went round talking to customers and bringing the work in. The money was superb and a big help in getting us back on our feet, but my heart wasn't in it. I was still hiding all the time and if I saw anybody from the Press I was embarrassed. I shouldn't have been because I was back up and earning more than them. And it had been hard: I had been so low that somebody else might have taken an overdose, but I'd done it. I should have been proud of that.

By doing bits on the side, I gradually worked my way back into the newspaper business, and I would have gone back into it full time much earlier if the money hadn't been so good with *Pimlico Plumbers*. In the end, I had to make a choice because I couldn't handle all the work. Although, there really was no choice because the newspaper business is my trade; it's *me*. When I first started working for the Press, at the same time as working for my brothers, it was still the 'old school' style of journalism. It has been part of my life for a very long time. People in the business sometimes ring up and ask if a particular story is mine, and I'll ask how they know because some papers don't give a by-line. They say they just recognise my style, and I get a kick out of that.

Having come through these experiences of losing everything and having to go out and strive to make money just to survive, I realise that there is some part of me that enjoys the challenge and the struggle. In some masochistic way, I like the uncertainty of not knowing what I'm going to do, or how I'll solve a problem. And if I don't have any problems to solve, I go looking for them. I'm thinking *all* the time, 24/7. Jeannette will often wake up and catch me lying there, staring at the ceiling, and she'll ask what I'm thinking about *now!* I might be inventing something, so, in effect, I've thought of a thing or a situation that could be improved and given myself the job of figuring it out. At the moment, I'm working on a surveillance idea involving helicopters.

Although I rarely follow through or get prototypes of my inventions made, I have often helped the companies I've worked for because I have a gift for being able to think of ways to make things easier or get over a problem. It might be a small thing but it increases efficiency. If I was younger, I could probably make a good living at it, but I'd be bored rigid very quickly.

Losing everything and being at survival level is problem solving in the extreme. It has been suggested that because I loved my childhood, when we had nothing and I was happy, I associate happiness with having nothing. It would take a psychiatrist to sort that one out, but it's an interesting idea. I would say it has more to do with the adrenalin rush of not having any money and then getting some.

I talk a lot about money because we have to have it to survive, so it's being at that point of not knowing how I'll survive, and then finding a way, that produces the adrenalin that is my drug of choice!

Money, in and of itself, is not important: it's no more than a means to an end; I like it but it's not my god, and I spend it or give it away without a thought when I've got it. Money is for spending: that's what they print it for. It would be a crime *not* to spend it! I'm not clever with money and I would never think of planning for the future – pensions, ISA's, all that – and maybe, for Jeannette's sake, I should, but I don't understand it and I glaze over at the mention of it; it bores me.

That may sound arrogant, but I actually just have a very low boredom threshold. Just recently, I started getting terrible tension headaches. I'm not worried about anything, yet I feel tense to the point of nausea. The doctor put me on a low dose of Valium, which stopped the pain behind my eyes; but, why am I worrying? *I'm* not worrying: my brain is! I'm not happy when there's nothing going on: it depresses me, which I think is adrenalin withdrawal. I've been addicted to that adrenalin rush all my life.

# 21
# Artistic Licence

I've loved art ever since I started mixing coloured inks – the dregs left at the bottom of containers - at the back of my brothers' shop when I was nine, but I did not have much opportunity to practice until we moved to Hatch End. I really got into it then, because there was more space and I had more scope for the things I wanted to do.

At first, I made wooden boxes and all sorts of things in the garage. I gave a lot away, but I had so many boxes that we got a weekly stall at Covent Garden for a while. Some of the boxes were just French polished with gold hinges and clasps; others, I textured with paper then painted with three layers of different colours, and, before varnishing, went over the box with wire wool so that the colours showed through; others, I painted flowers on in unusual ways, or aged with a process I worked out that didn't involve expensive ageing fluid. I also did découpage on one, although I didn't know that was what I was doing until somebody told me!

I've never been taught. I've just done whatever I liked, or whatever came to me, and used whatever materials I had to hand. I've experimented. I bought some oil paint once and decided it was a waste of money and took so long to dry that I would make something equivalent, myself. I got some emulsion and tried different powders in it, like bicarbonate of soda and talcum powder, to see how much I could build it up to look like oil paint. Nothing was any good until I found whiting, which is the actual compound used in paint. My father used it make paint from scratch when he was painting and decorating; all paint is made with it. You can only get it in craft shops now at some inflated price. However, I bought some, mixed it and mixed it, leaving a couple of hours in between each mix, and it ended up like oil paint: I could mix it on my palette, work with it and mould it as I pleased, and it took hours instead of days to dry.

When I hadn't got anything else, I worked out ways to use paper, which I love; I buy reams of non-acid tissue paper. I crush a length of it, dip it in water and then spread it on a board. The water holds it to the board and makes it moveable so that I can create forms or textures, which I then very gently paint with emulsion to make it all hard; tissue paper with emulsion dries rock solid. Sometimes, I paint the paper with a colour first and then do my scrunching. After that, I paint however or whatever I want on it. But again, I don't use expensive tubes of oil paint: I buy odd tins of paints that people have had mixed and then don't like; the shop is glad to get rid of them and I get them for a quarter of the price. Then I mix those colours to get what I want. A friend saw some of this type of picture and asked me to texture his whole hall and stairway in the same way, which I did, and he's kept it that way. There are unexpected shapes in it – like a face, maybe - that you don't see at first, so it's interesting to look at.

I've never pursued art seriously. I do it for the love of it. But I've had a couple of commissions: one was for the owner of a new mansion. I showed him a picture I called *Cornfield* and he asked me to do a very large version – about eight feet by six - to hang in the stairwell of his house. I didn't do it on canvas because it would have cost hundreds of pounds for a picture that big. I painted it on a dustsheet! I stretched the sheet on a frame, which I also made myself, and painted it with PVA glue so that it stiffened up, then I stretched and painted it again until it stayed smooth. Over that, I painted white emulsion and after it dried I painted the picture. It was like painting on wood.

I actually do sculptures on wood. Years ago, when we moved from Hatch End to the house we have now, I had a big shed built in the garden - or a 'studio', as Jeannette calls it - and started sculpting, as well. To commemorate the Queen's jubilee, I made a piece I called *Jubilee* from cement and concrete on a board base; it's so heavy it takes at least two men to lift it. It's an abstract of flags and different style London houses - both old-fashioned and modern - with the odd little surprise, like a fireplace, suddenly hitting the eye. I've never done anything with it; I just did it because it came to me, like all the rest.

I did another, on wood, of an old-fashioned football boot, which was later displayed at the Football Association building in Lancaster Gate. I took it to show them and they liked it; it was on display for over a year.

I can look at a piece of clay and not know what I'm going to do with it. I don't have to. I mould it and mess about with it and see what shapes present themselves, like a possible tree or a foot, then I work

273

with it. I love it! I could do one every day. Some of the free-standing sculpture I've done includes a series of anthropomorphised animals: a rhino carrying a gun and dressed in safari gear; a rodent in a coat and shoes, one with a hole in it; a lion dressed as royalty, just to name a few. I give them away, throw them away, put them all over the house, and the loft is still full of pictures and sculptures.

When Laura was little, I would tell her to roll up all her plasticine, mould it, then look at it and decide what it looked like. She'd see something in it and I'd say, 'Well, let's make that.' You have to have the eye for it; I don't believe that can be taught. I think it's fantastic to be able to see a suggestion of something and then make it happen.

That's how the piece I have on display in NATO came about. During the Serbian-Croatian-Bosnian war I was at a NATO press conference, and I saw a plaque of the NATO sign with the hand and the dove. A while later, Jeannette and I were walking the dog across the fields behind the house, and I saw some barbed wire. Thinking it was dangerous and could hurt Sunny, my dog, I went to pick it up and as I did I got an idea. I had already done a sculpture of Jeannette's and my hands and it had taken ages but I decided to try something similar: I made a plaque with barbed wire at the base of two hands. I didn't do anything with it until a friend happened to comment that it would be good for NATO. I said they had already got one of their own, but he insisted that it was very timely, in light of the war. So I took a picture of it and emailed it to them. Two or three weeks later I got an email back, saying they loved the sculpture and could they see it.

It was very heavy, which I told them, so they paid for it to go over by courier. I expected to get it back, but I later got an email to say that it was hanging in the Press area of their offices in Brussels. I immediately rang them and asked them to send me a picture of it in situ, thinking they might throw it away when they took it down. During that conversation they asked if they could keep it. Automatically, I started thinking of the money I could get for it, and I actually hesitated! But they only had to point out what a wonderful gift it would be to NATO and I agreed. I still have the letter they sent, thanking me.

Yet, I can really put myself down sometimes: I actually wondered why they would want my piece on the wall. I was proud of doing it, proud to give it to NATO, proud that they wanted it and proud that my name was underneath it, but I didn't understand why I was proud because I didn't think it should be me: I thought maybe it should be somebody very intelligent. I don't know why I feel that.

It was the same the first time I was asked to exhibit my stuff in the McNeill Masters Art Gallery in Radlett. I was at a Press event, chatting to a lady who told me she had an art gallery. I mentioned that I liked art and did a bit but only played at it, to which she replied that she'd like to see my 'playing'. I was surprised that she was willing to come all the way to my house, but she subsequently came for supper with her partner.

When I took them into my garage, I wondered what on earth I thought I was doing, but they were knocked out. I had a sculpture of a saxophonist, which was another one where I'd been creative with the materials: it's a big piece and would have been very awkward to fire if I had made it out of clay, so I made it out of builders' bonding, which I then covered in plaster. The hands were based on my own little stumpy hands, which I drew first and then copied. They thought I had painted over a real saxophone. Then there was a three-dimensional picture of a large sunflower with lots of smaller ones in the background that they thought was fabulous, despite the fact it was all covered in dust! Anyway, she said I had enough for an exhibition. I thought she was taking the piss! But she priced everything and it all went ahead; amongst other things, I sold the saxophonist for twelve hundred pounds.

Somebody was taking pictures of one of my sculptures at this exhibition – a piece called *Carnival* – and I was subsequently asked if they could put the picture in their magazine, *Optima*. Naturally, I said yes.

I also got a call from the gallery owner who said that an insurance company had seen my work and wanted me to sculpt fruit over an entire section of a restaurant they were opening. I did apples, bananas and all the rest, and added touches like cut up tomatoes with the seeds falling out, all of which they were very pleased with, which pleased me too.

All of that is lovely, and I'm happy and grateful when people take pleasure in my art, but that's not why I do it, or I would be disappointed more often than not and probably stop!

I see art in everyday things. We have acres and acres of fields around our house, and I was walking Sunny, one day, when I saw three or four old rusting Coke tins. They spoiled the beauty so I picked them up and as I did an idea came to me. I collected fir cones, bits of bark and all kinds of plants and greenery, took it all home and made a collage of all the beautiful things in Nature, marred by rusty old cans.

A lot of people look at that, and, for some reason, don't understand it. When that happens, it puts me off and I think maybe it's crap and I might throw it away. I'm a child in that way, because I'm passionate about everything I do, and when somebody puts a blot on it or mars it with a comment, I leave it and never go back to it. People have different tastes, of course, and I accept that. If somebody says something I've done is no good, based on dislike or lack of understanding, though, I get annoyed. That's a judgement I don't believe anyone has the right to make.

Art is simply there in the background of my life. I love it and would do so much more, if I had the time.

# 22
# The Fat Lady Hasn't Sung

I'm still an investigator, and I still work closely with the newspapers. Just recently, Blake Fielder-Civil, Amy Winehouse's husband, was sentenced to twenty seven months in prison for perverting the course of justice by trying to buy a barman's silence, after having beaten him up. I became involved in that story, and later, the court case, when a middle man, Anthony Kelly, who called himself Ant, contacted the *Mirror*, saying he had CCTV footage of Amy Winehouse's husband and another guy beating the crap out of a barman. He said no one else had seen this footage, so the *Mirror* thought there might be a story in it.

Stephen Moyes, the journalist I was working with, and I checked out the footage: the barman wasn't visible, but Fielder-Civil was talking to someone in a doorway and suddenly rushed forward and joined in a fight; the screen was full of arms and legs flying; then we could see Fielder-Civil and another guy kicking somebody senseless, but not who it was.

This fellow, Ant, was friendly with the beaten barman, James King, and had suggested to him that they talk to Fielder-Civil and get some money for keeping their mouths shut, but he was playing two sides against the middle: he didn't tell James King that he had approached the *Mirror* with this story, and we didn't know that Ant was actually planning to take the money-for-silence from Fielder-Civil.

As far as we were concerned, Ant was setting King and Fielder-Civil up, and selling us the story of Amy Winehouse's husband trying to pervert the course of justice: basically, turning them over.

Ant arranged a meeting with James King at a certain address to discuss approaching Fielder-Civil for money. I went in beforehand and put in surveillance equipment: a camera and audio hidden in a handbag, and a PIR (passive infrared detector) on the wall, transmitting audio and video to a receiver and recorder hidden behind the sofa in the next room. I told Ant I was switching the cameras on and leaving them running so that he would not have to touch anything, and then I went outside to wait with Stephen.

King arrived, discussed the plot with Ant and then left. We retrieved the footage and part of it showed Ant approaching the PIR and turning the camera off! He had misunderstood me and thought he was switching it on! So we got nothing from that camera. However, we did get everything on the camera in the handbag. It wasn't as good quality as it might have been, but it was all there.

A day or so later, we went to meet Ant at the flat of a friend of his in Camden, which is the area where Fielder-Civil and Amy Winehouse live, and Ant rang Fielder-Civil to suggest a meeting. It came to nothing because Fielder-Civil was very evasive, so we shelved all that until the next day. As we were leaving, however, I noticed a box that looked familiar to me, and I asked him about it. He opened it, and it was some of the same kind of investigative equipment as I have – a shirt with a camera in one of the buttons and a recorder. He said he had bought it, but I was suspicious: this was expensive equipment and it was much more likely that a newspaper had given it to him to use.

When we got outside, I mentioned this to Stephen, and he told me that Ant had originally taken the idea to *News of the World*, but they hadn't been interested. Ant was just a villain and I thought he might be trying to sell the story to both the *Mirror* and *News of the World*. We decided that if we wanted an exclusive, we would have to find a way to 'keep him on side' and convince him it was in his own best interests not to fall out of favour with us.

A call to Ant followed and when I said I had a proposition to put to him it was not difficult to arrange an immediate meeting. We met at his house and he asked if I would mind walking his dog with him. So there we were, walking the dog while I buttered his ego, telling him I was freelance and there would be jobs he could help me with. I mentioned using prostitutes as informants and he said he knew quite a few of them; that convinced him we were both on the same side. At this point, I was still protecting a story and had not realised how far Ant was planning to go.

The next night, Stephen and I met with him and his driver (Ant was banned from driving) and equipped them both: Ant with a tie and the driver with a coat, both of which had a camera and audio sewn into them. This time, Fielder-Civil had agreed to meet with Ant at a pub close to Fielder-Civil's home, and we got all the recorded footage of them talking about the deal.

After that meeting, Ant went off to get a signed statement from the barman saying he would lie for Fielder-Civil. He came back a couple of hours later with a video on his phone, in which King was holding up a piece of paper and saying it was a statement that he would change his evidence against Fielder-Civil. Ant needed that to convince Fielder-Civil that it was a bona fide deal with King, since King had never taken part in the negotiations himself. Ant later gave us the signed statement to photocopy and include in the story to appear in the newspaper.

This all happened over the course of four or five days, enough time for us to come to the gradual realisation that Ant and his driver were intending to take the money. At that point, we informed the police, and they set up a trap at a Canary Wharf pub.

It was a lovely sunny day, and Stephen met with Ant and his driver, supposedly to discuss payment for the story. Having done that, Stephen left, saying he was going to get his boss and bring him to the meeting. This was the moment for the police to swoop in. It all turned a bit of messy because Ant tried to fight his way out of it, and it took quite a few police officers to hold him down.

I was later called to testify because I had all the incriminating footage.

The type of surveillance equipment I used in gathering evidence for that story is typical of the equipment my company custom makes to order. We can put equipment into anything the client wants, and the range of the equipment can be such that people in another country can be watched.

Before I formed my own company, I worked for an ex-policeman, and one of the places we worked was 'air-side' at Heathrow (areas not open to the travelling public). I don't remember the year, but it was the time of – although not connected with - the IRA troubles, and we worked there for quite some time.

On one occasion, I had to put cameras above the urinals in the gents' toilets because the money put into condom machines was being stolen. This amounts to a lot of money because condoms aren't available in certain countries, so men stock up on them!

Bradley, my son-in-law, was helping me to position the cameras and he hid in one of the cubicles to avoid suspicion of 'wrongdoing' if anyone came into any of the toilets. In one of them, I crawled gingerly along the inside of the suspended ceiling, which was not meant to take the weight of a person, and inadvertently knelt on a screw that was sticking up; it went right into my knee. I screamed, jerked to the side, broke the ceiling, fell halfway through and ended up hanging suspended over two poor blokes having a pee! They thought I was a pervert! After Bradley and I sorted all that out, fixed the ceiling and got the cameras in, we discovered that it was the cleaners who were ransacking the machines.

We caught people doing all kinds of things.

Running my own company, there were many instances of working with husbands or wives whose spouse was 'over the side' - in other words, having an affair. One man, whose wife suspected him and wanted her suspicions checked out, had a pied à terre in London – the ideal place to conduct an affair. We made use of the fact that the cleaning woman only came in weekly by putting a camera in the vacuum cleaner. For one thing, the batteries in our equipment would recharge every time it was turned on; for another, we didn't expect him to do anything with it! Unfortunately, he did move it, and then left it somewhere so that we were looking at the bloody wall! As luck would have it, a woman came and moved it; we saw her legs and, as she moved away, her face, so we had him!

A funny incident was when a man came to us suspecting his wife of having an affair. When he found out he was right, he didn't mind because it was with a woman. He was quite happy with that. If it had been a man, he would have felt differently.

On the opposite side of the fence, we do a lot of sweeping of buildings, using equipment that can detect most bugs. The exception is a new type that works on a form of mobile phone: the bug is triggered when someone dials the number; if no one has dialled the number, the bug can't be found. While we check everywhere, including the walls, we have another little machine that has a television with two aerials; if anybody is using a remote camera, like the ones we use, the picture of what it's focused on comes up on our little machine.

More often than not, when we do a sweep, we don't find anything - it's just people being paranoid - but we did one for a very well known building supply company and we found three bugs, two of which were in directors' chairs. The bugs only had eight day batteries in them, which meant that whoever had put them there had to come back to change the batteries. The obvious thing was to put cameras in to find out who it was. The managing director immediately put himself under suspicion by not allowing this. We put *him* under surveillance, checked his computer files when he wasn't there, and found out that he was the guilty party. The reason was that the company was being taken over and he wasn't privy to all the meetings going on at the highest level. He wanted to know which company was ahead in the bidding war so that he could buy shares in that company. He was the one who had actually called us in, in the first place, thinking it would divert any possible suspicion from himself. He was stupid!

We also found a couple of bugs in a hedge fund company in the City and saved them a *lot* of money. The bugs were transmitting from their boardrooms to a mini cab office across the road. The mini cab company was implicated because they were letting someone use one of their rooms. The only thing in it was a recorder.

It's a fascinating business. A Russian oligarch was a bit worried, called us in, and we found a bug in the brickwork of the house he was having built. Because it was all in process, whoever had placed the bug had been able to remove a brick, drill a hole through it, just stopping at coming out the other side, put pinholes in the remaining skin of brick and the bug behind them. That could have stayed transmitting from the house forever because it could have been connected to the electrics. We never found out who had put it there, but it didn't stay there!

I love life, but maybe I've seen too much, heard too much and dug up too much crap, because I believe it's a shit world we live in - a dog eat dog world. If you don't shit on somebody, they will shit on you first. Even if you're a nice person with the slippers and the Sunday roast before going back to work on Monday, there's still somebody shitting on you from a great height – your boss, the government, or both – and you think you're happy because you've got a job, you're paying your mortgage, you're going out for a ride on your bike with your wife, and it's all very nice. Me, I'd rather hang myself than live that kind of life! But whoever you are, you are being shit on; you only have to look at the world.

If you just sit there, waiting, you will be very lucky if something comes along or someone gives you something. Nothing changes unless you change it yourself. You've got to contribute something to get something back, even if that something is not very nice. Needs must when the devil drives, and if you need money you have to go out and find a way of earning it. That's all I've done, and I will do anything (apart from sell my body!), even wash cars or sweep the streets. I think it would really hurt me, but I'd do those things if I had to because I'm not proud; pride doesn't pay the mortgage or put food on the table.

Nobody gave me anything. My parents tried and they couldn't; they gave me life and looked after me, but there was no money and that was fine. All my family clawed their way up to have a good life. If we could do it, coming from the slums with no advantages whatsoever, anybody can. If I'd have been a nine to five man and kept the money I've earned, Jeannette and I would definitely be millionaires by now - probably only one million, but we would have done it. Instead, we've had a fantastic life.

At sixty one, I look at myself in the mirror and think, *who's going to want me now? If what I'm doing, now, comes to an end, what will I do?*

Then again, when I have a few days of the phone not ringing and nothing much happening, I think maybe I'm too old and I should be acting my age, thinking about giving up and getting out the pipe and slippers. But it doesn't appeal, and I wouldn't know how. I don't act my age because I'm too much of a live wire. Sometimes, I look at myself all dressed up – 'mutton dressed as lamb', my mum would say – and wonder what I'm doing, but I love all that, so I carry on. I may not be here tomorrow.

My life in a nutshell:
    I can resist everything except temptation.
                        -    Oscar Wilde

287